Colin Smith

Peachpit Press

How to Wow with Flash
Colin Smith

Peachpit Press
1249 Eighth Street
Berkeley, CA 94710
510/524-2178
510/524-2221 (fax)

Find us on the Web at: www.peachpit.com
To report errors, please send a note to errata@peachpit.com

Peachpit Press is a division of Pearson Education

Editors: Rebecca Gulick and Matthew Purcell
Production Coordinator: David Van Ness
Proofreader: Liz Welch
Technical Editor: Matt Keefe
Compositor: Colin Smith
Indexer: Karin Arrigoni
Cover design: Jack Davis
Interior design: Jill Davis

ISBN 0-321-42649-5
9 8 7 6 5 4 3
Printed and bound in the United States of America

Acknowledgments

First of all, I want to thank you, the reader, for buying this book! Without you and the hundreds of thousands of people who visit my website, buy my books and videos, and attend my seminars, I would be digging holes on the side of the road somewhere for a living!

Although I'm the lead author on this book, it was far from a solo effort. So many good people were involved in the creation of this book and I want to give a little shout out to some of them.

Thank you to Jack Davis for having the faith in me to author such an exciting and important addition to your brilliant How to Wow series. It's important for the Flash community of designers looking for inspiration and ideas with Flash 8 and important to the masses of people who are wanting to get into Flash in a non-intimidating way. Thanks for taking the time in Boston to brainstorm and get this book kicked off, and thanks to your partner, Jill, for her excellent design work on this series.

Thanks to all the friends I have at Adobe, especially Gwen Weisberg, Addy Roff, Julieanne Kost, John Nack, Jeff Tranberry, and others. Your support over the years has really been appreciated. Keep making these awesome products!

Thanks a ton to my friends who have contributed to these pages. Chris Georgenos, it was great hanging out in L.A. Thanks for taking the time to lend your talents to this project. Michael Donnellan, thanks for your help and inspiration. Also, thanks to Matt Keefe for the contributions, speedy tech edits, and countless phone calls discussing arrays, XML nodes, and attributes.

I have to thank Mauriahh Beezley for her help with all the corrections in the book. Thanks for giving up your time to get everything done on time.

Ali Sabet and Philip J. Neal, thanks for contributing some of your excellent artwork for some of the projects in this book.

It wouldn't have been possible without some of the talent and faces of friends that endured the hot lights in my little garage in California. Thanks to Christie for dancing for the camera; to Kuntal, Angela, Mauriahh, Michael, and Kaysar for standing so still as I fiddled with the settings and lighting to get the photographs that I needed and for lending your faces for my lens.

I truly appreciate the hard work that Brie Gyncild has put in. Thanks for watching hours of video and turning it into such eloquently written words for this book.

A big thanks to all the folks at Peachpit Press for working so hard on this project to make it a reality. To Nancy Ruenzel, Rebecca Gulick, Matt Purcell, David Van Ness, Liz Welch, Becky Morgan, and all the other friends that I have at Peachpit, thanks for having faith in me and keep on producing the best computer books in the world!

Thanks to all the gang at Software Cinema, Gary, David, Nathaniel, Chris, Lisa, and Brooke. I'm looking forward to the DVDs and future tours. It's great to partner with you on this project.

Cheers to Gabriel at B&H for always steering me in the right direction and making sure I get the right gear for the job.

Thanks to my buddies in the industry. Al Ward from actionfx.com, it's been a pleasure working with you and co-authoring a few titles over the years, I'm grateful for your friendship.

My buddies at NAPP, Scott, Dave, Matt, Jeff, Chris, Melinda, and a whole bunch more of you, I always enjoy working with you guys. Your spirit of sharing is inspirational as well as refreshing in a dog-eat-dog world.

Michael Ninness, Lynda, and Bruce at Lynda.com, thanks for the talks, support, and for putting on the great Flash Forward Conferences.

A shout out to my chess buddies Brad and Adrian. Thanks for all the games that help keep my mind sharp and that distract me from my real work.

I have so many more people that I would love to mention and thank. These few columns are not enough, but you know who you are!

Thanks to God for giving me the talent and creativity I need and allowing me to have so much fun and call it work!

—*Colin Smith*

Contents

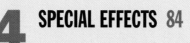

9 DYNAMIC APPLICATIONS 204

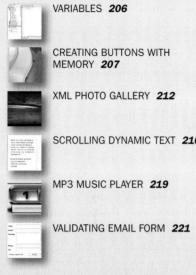

Introduction

OVER THE LAST FEW YEARS, we have seen a huge boom in multimedia and web development. Right in the middle of the explosion is an application that is arguably the most fun to work with in the world. Yep, you guessed it: Flash!

What started as a humble animation program has transformed the electronic world and created a culture of design fanatics called Flashers (people who use Flash to create stunning animations and interactive applications). It's not hard to see why. Just look at the kinds of things that people are doing in Flash. Exciting pages are springing up all over the Web. Almost every movie and music artist's website is created in Flash. Why? Because where else will you get such a compelling, interactive multimedia experience that includes motion graphics, effects, music, video, and sound? It's easy to see why so many people choose Flash and I know that you, like me, are drawn like a moth to a flame to this exciting desktop application.

Flash has really grown up in the latest version. Not only can we create sweeping motion, jaw-dropping effects and

fully interactive applications, we can now add intelligent video and do it with ease! Flash 8 is jammed full of new features for designers and we will use most of these features throughout this book.

Why Do You Need This Book?

When people see the amazing work that is being created with Flash, they can't help but be impressed. Inspired to create similar work, they rush out, buy Flash, tear open the box, and install the application on their machine, all the time drooling over the exciting work they will create in the first five minutes. Then, horror takes over. This isn't as easy as they thought. What are all these menus, and this ActionScript thing? Flash can be a very intimidating and difficult program for the beginning user.

That's why this How to Wow book exists. Perhaps you have learned some of the basics and you are fairly comfortable with the basic interface, but you can't for the life of you create anything that looks visually cool. You have tried to find the answers and techniques for the amazing effects that drew you to the program, only to find that the secrets are closely sealed up in the minds of a few.

The goal of this book is to burst the dam that has held you back. In it, I reveal

the secrets that I have learned over the years, including the most requested and guarded techniques. Be frustrated no more. The mantra of How to Wow is "Quality, Flexibility and Speed," which you will experience for yourself as you work through the pages of this book.

Prepare to smile with a deep sense of satisfaction as you begin to re-create the effects you have seen on the hottest sites and projects.

This is not an ActionScript book. In the pages and on the disc I have included all the ActionScript you need to finish all the projects and use the results. However, I haven't devoted too much space to learning ActionScript, which is a discipline in itself. The scope of this book should equip the average designer

fairly well, but if you are hungry for more, there are plenty of books written on ActionScript. (I have a dozen or so on my bookshelf.) To get the most out of Flash, I recommend reading a good beginning ActionScript book after you complete this book.

What this book will show you is how to create stunning effects quickly and easily. This volume is jam-packed with so many mouth-watering recipes—about 60 of them, in fact. I have spent years accumulating the knowledge that you now hold in your hands. I wish I could go back in time and lay my hands on this book!

What's on the CD-ROM?

To make your experience as enjoyable and trouble-free as possible, I ask that you NOT give into the temptation to skip the first chapter before you dive into all the fun stuff in later chapters.

There is some valuable information in the first chapter that will help you throughout the rest of the book.

The CD-ROM at the back of the book contains all the files you need to follow along with the projects. There are also end files for each project to give you a sense of where you're going and for you to use in troubleshooting your own projects.

You will also find some really useful applications on the disc, which you'll learn how to configure in Chapter 9. These applications will enable you to implement XML photo galleries that are truly dynamic. You will be able to create email forms, digital jukeboxes, and more. These are the kinds of things that you could spend a lot of time trying to track down and even longer trying to figure them out. But they are included right on the How to Wow CD.

Finally, if you have any questions about the book or problems with the CD-ROM, contact Peachpit Press at ask@peachpit.com.

Enjoy! 🎬

1

MASTERING THE BASICS

This chapter will get you up to speed with the basics of Flash 8.

WIND SPEED: CHECK. Flaps: check. Radio: check. Before taking off for some exotic and distant destination, a pilot will always run a preflight check just to make sure everything is okay. A good pilot also creates a flight plan and knows exactly where to fly and how to get there. The fact that you have resisted the urge to jump into the juiciest projects and are reading this introduction tells me that you want to know where you are going before you hit the throttle and speed down the runway.

Before we dive into all the exciting things like motion, video, sound and ActionScript-controlled wizardry, let's get started with a few of the basics. These are the building blocks that everything else is based on. In this chapter, you will be working with symbols, instances, and shapes. You will use tweens to breathe life into these objects and propel them across your screen.

You will not only learn how to move things on the Timeline, you will also learn how to make things morph and shape-shift. You will use instances to build up complex graphics while keeping file size as small as possible. Learning the difference

between instances and symbols is fundamental in understanding how Flash works. Use these techniques to create efficient files that can be controlled by ActionScript later on.

It's very helpful to know the difference between frames and keyframes and when to use which. Although slightly, keyframes add to the file size, so let's keep those to a minimum.

With Flash 8 Professional, not only do you have filters now, but you also have the ability to animate them and to change them over time. We will be making a helicopter take off and reproduce a very lifelike shadow effect. This kind of thing was never possible in Flash before without creating a huge file size and wasting a lot of time.

You will also learn how to animate different parts of movie clips independently to each other. This skill is necessary to build complex-looking animations.

I'm going to step outside the obvious areas of the interface to show you how to set up a page to detect whether a viewer has the latest version of the Flash Player installed—and to direct them to a download if not. I'll also walk you through creating multimedia projects for CD or DVD using Flash.

You can control how the screen looks, even displaying the project full-screen with no bars around the edges. For those members of your audience who want to have some control, you'll learn how to make a quit button that lets them escape the full-screen nirvana.

With a program as exciting as Flash is, even the basics aren't boring. Come along and get your flight plan in place, so you can soar your way through this book and countless future Flash projects.

Symbols

Symbols keep file sizes small and give you access to filters, blending modes, and ActionScript.

About Symbols

One of the advantages of Flash is that you can create robust, interesting animations without sacrificing small file sizes and quick download times. Symbols are the key. No matter how many times you use a symbol in a project, Flash includes the object's data in the file only once. This is particularly important in animation, where the same object appears on many frames. Convert shapes or graphics into symbols before you animate multiple instances of them in Flash.

Symbols are stored in the Library panel. When you drag a symbol to the stage, the original remains in the library, and an instance appears in your project. You can create as many instances as you want. There are three kinds of symbols in Flash: movie clip, button, and graphic. How you can work with a symbol depends on which kind of symbol it is. In the library, the symbol type appears next to the symbol's name. You can tell whether an instance is a button, movie clip, or graphic by selecting it on the stage and looking in the Properties Inspector.

Converting Objects to Symbols

There are several ways to convert an object to a symbol:

- Select the object, and choose Modify > Convert to Symbol.
- Right-click the object and choose Convert to Symbol.
- Select the object and press the F8 key. Flash opens the Convert to Symbol dialog box. Select a type for the symbol (movie clip, button, or graphic), and name it.

Click in the registration grid to set the registration point, the point Flash will use as a reference for positioning, rotating, or resizing the symbol. If you're planning to rotate the graphic and want it to stay in place as it rotates, select the center registration point. Otherwise, it's usually best to select the upper-left corner so you have the most control over positioning and resizing the symbol.

If you need to access other settings, click Advanced.

Movie Clip Symbols

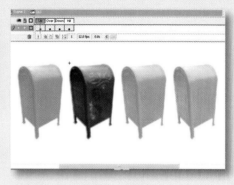

Movie clip symbols are ideal for animation. They have their own multiframe timeline that is independent from the main timeline. Movie clip timelines can contain interactive controls, sounds, and even other movie clip instances. Movie clip symbols are the most flexible symbols in Flash. You can attach filters to a movie clip symbol, as well as color settings and blending modes. You can name movie clip instances and control them with Action-Script. And you can apply runtime bitmap caching to smooth playback.

When you select Movie Clip for the Type in the Convert to Symbol dialog box, the Export for ActionScript option becomes available. Flash uses the movie clip's name as the identifier by default.

Button Symbols

If you're creating simple buttons or invisible buttons, button symbols can save you time. Button symbol timelines don't play like movie clip timelines; instead, they provide rollover states that you can define to easily create interactive buttons.

The rollover states in the button symbol's timeline have specific functions:

- The Up state is the default state, shown whenever the pointer is not over the button.

- The Over state is the button's appearance when the pointer is over the button.

- The Down state is the button's appearance when it is clicked.

- The Hit state defines the button's active area, the area that responds to the mouse click.

You can name button instances, and apply ActionScript to them. You can also apply filters, blending modes, and color settings.

Graphic Symbols

Graphic symbols are best used for static images that you want to reuse multiple times, such as background images. You may also use graphic symbols to create pieces of animation connected to the main timeline, but interactive controls and sounds won't work in a graphic symbol's animation. If you're just creating simple motion tweens, graphic symbols work great.

In general, graphic symbols are much less flexible than movie clip symbols. You cannot apply filters or blending modes to a graphic symbol. Nor can you name its instances and apply ActionScript to it. ▥

INSIGHT

Movie Clips as Buttons. As you'll see later in the book, many Flash designers prefer to use movie clip symbols to create buttons, so they can add more complex and smoother animation. If you're creating basic buttons for a simple site, use a button symbol. If you're creating something more unusual or want a subtler effect, consider using a movie clip symbol instead.

Motion Tweening

Let Flash create motion animation frames for you, so you can focus on the big picture—and keep your file size small.

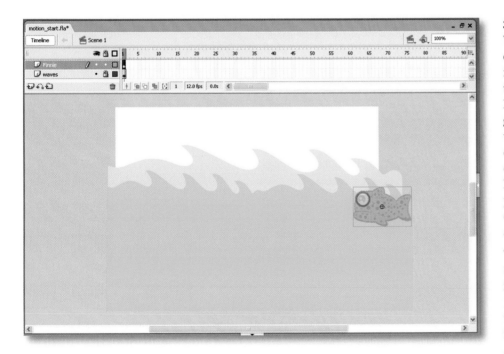

1. Create a Keyframe

With motion tweening, you define properties such as position, size, and rotation for an instance at one keyframe, and then change those properties at another. Flash creates the intermediate steps to generate the animation. In this project, we'll move Finnie, our fish friend, from one side of the stage to the other. I've opened the Motion_start.fla file from the How to Wow CD (motionstart.tif). The project includes two layers, one that contains the waves in the background and one that contains Finnie.

There is one frame in the timeline; by default, it's a keyframe. The frame rate is 12 frames per second (fps), so at frame 12, approximately one second of animation will have passed. We'd like Finnie to take three seconds to cross the stage. At 12 fps, three seconds of animation is approximately 36 frames. Select frame 36 in the Finnie layer and press F6 to create a keyframe.

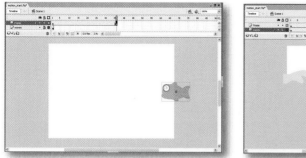

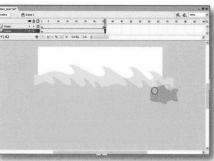

2. Add Frames for the Waves

The Finnie layer now has 36 frames in it, with a keyframe at frame 36. But the background doesn't show up at frame 36. That's because the Waves layer has only one frame. Flash only displays content as long as there's a frame in the layer. So let's add frames to the Waves layer. We aren't animating the waves, so we only need frames, not a keyframe. Select frame 36 in the Waves layer and press F5. Flash fills in all the frames with the content that was on the first frame.

3. Create the Motion Tween

Finnie's going to start on the right side of the stage and move to the left. Select the keyframe on frame 36 of the Finnie layer. Then, move Finnie to his final position at the left side of the stage. Hold down the Shift key as you move him to constrain the movement so that it's perfectly horizontal. Now if you scrub through the timeline, Finnie is on the right side of the stage until frame 36, when he jumps to the left. We want him to move across the stage over 36 frames. Select the first keyframe in the Finnie layer, and then choose Motion from the Tween menu in the Properties Inspector.

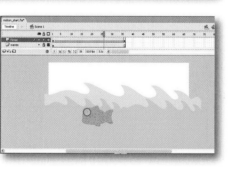

Now Flash displays an arrow in the timeline to show that the animation is tweened, and when you scrub through the timeline, you see Finnie swim across the stage. To see Finnie in action, press Ctrl+Enter (Windows) or Cmd+Return (Mac OS) to preview the movie.

> **T I P**
>
> **Scrub the Timeline.** Moving the playhead is called scrubbing. As you scrub through the timeline, Flash displays each frame, including any animation.

> **T I P**
>
> **Shortcut to Tween.** If you don't want to open the Properties Inspector to create a motion tween, just right-click (Windows) or Control-click (Mac OS) any frame between the keyframes, and choose Create Motion Tween.

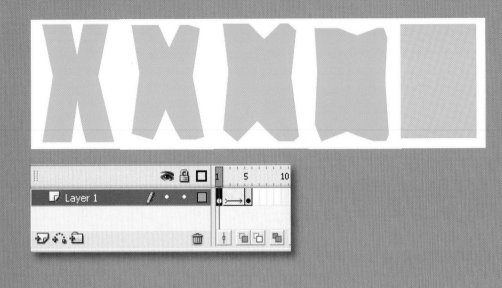

Shape Tweening

Morph shapes almost magically. You create the beginning and end shapes, and Flash takes care of the middle.

1. Create the Initial Shape

A shape tween is like a motion tween in that you create the beginning and end shapes and Flash fills in the intermediate steps. But unlike a motion tween, the object isn't just changing position, color, or angle—it's actually turning into something else, what the science fiction crowd call shape-shifting. Unlike motion tweening, which works best with symbols, you actually want to use shape tweening with the original vector artwork. Let's create a fun, simple shape tween to get you started.

Open a new document in Flash. We'll create a simple object, the letter "X." Select the Text tool, and set the text properties, such as font, in the Properties Inspector. Type in a large text size. I'm using 250-point Impact type for a nice blocky shape.

To convert the text to a vector shape, so we can use a shape tween, press Ctrl+B (Windows) or Cmd+B (Mac OS).

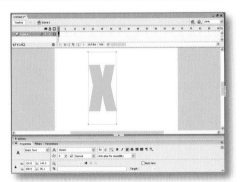

T I P

Break It Up. If you want to tween the shape of a symbol or text, break it apart by selecting it and pressing Ctrl+B (Windows) or Cm+B (Mac OS). Shape tweening only works on vector shapes.

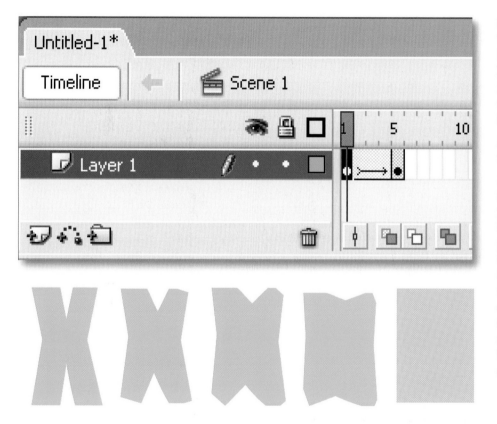

2. Create the Final Shape

We'll start with an "X" and morph it into a rectangle across five frames. So, select frame 5 and press F6 to create a keyframe. Select the Rectangle tool, with Object Drawing turned off, and draw a rectangle over the X on the stage.

3. Create a Shape Tween

We have the first shape on the first keyframe and the last shape on the last keyframe. We're just missing the middle frames. Select the first keyframe, and choose Shape from the Tween menu in the Properties Inspector.

An arrow appears between the keyframes in the timeline.

As you scrub through the timeline, the X morphs into a rectangle. To preview the animation, press the Enter key. To see a more accurate preview, publish the movie by pressing Ctrl+Enter (Windows) or Cmd+Return (Mac OS). Tweening gets its name from the animation industry. In the days of hand-drawn frames, the frames that signified key action points were created by the lead artists. The in-between frames were created by tween or in-between artists. 🎞

INSIGHT

Keep on Going. You're not limited to one change. A shape tween can also change color, position, rotation, and all the other attributes a motion tween affects. See what happens if you create a keyframe at frame 10, and draw a red oval over the rectangle. Experiment!

Working with Instances

When you drag a symbol to the stage, it becomes an instance of the symbol—and it's related to all other instances of the same symbol.

About Instances

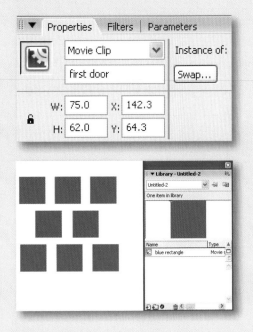

An instance is a copy of a symbol. You can have one instance of a symbol, hundreds, or none. No matter how many instances of a symbol you use in a project, Flash only needs to include the data for the symbol once, so the file size is much smaller than it might otherwise be.

You can name instances of movie clip and button symbols, and you can apply ActionScript to them. You can animate instances of any type of symbol by modifying them frame by frame, or by using motion tweens.

Instances remain related to the symbol. If you edit the symbol, all the instances of that symbol are affected. However, you can make changes to an individual instance without affecting other instances or the symbol.

Modifying Instances

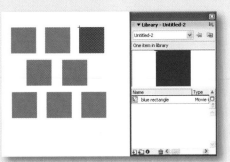

Whether changes affect only a single instance or all instances depends on how you make the changes.

Double-click on an instance to edit the symbol. Any changes you make to the symbol affect all instances of that symbol. To keep an instance from changing with the symbol, convert it to a drawn shape by selecting it and pressing Ctrl+B (Windows) or Cmd+B (Mac OS). When it's a drawn shape, it's independent of the symbol, but you also lose the advantage of reusing it without increasing file size, and you can no longer apply ActionScript or filters to it.

To change an instance without affecting other instances, select it and make changes in the Properties Inspector. You can 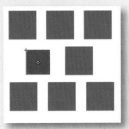 change the type of symbol (movie clip, button, or graphic), name the instance, change color settings, change the opacity, apply a blending mode, apply a filter (movie clips or buttons only), or change its size. ▥

Nesting Movie Clips

Life isn't simple, and your animations don't have to be either. Nesting movie clips is an easy way to build complex animations.

1. Position the Symbols

We'll animate a helicopter to move across the stage, but to make it more interesting and more realistic, we'll also animate the rotor and the tail rotor so that they're spinning simultaneously. Open the Helicopter_start.fla file from the How to Wow CD. The library contains three symbols: the chopper itself, the rotor, and the tail rotor, all drawn in Illustrator by my friend Philip Neal. Drag each symbol on the stage and assemble the helicopter.

The initial helicopter is too big for this stage. With the Selection tool, select all three instances.

Using the Free Transform tool, scale the helicopter and move it to the lower-right corner of the stage. Hold down the Shift key as you scale the helicopter to keep it proportional.

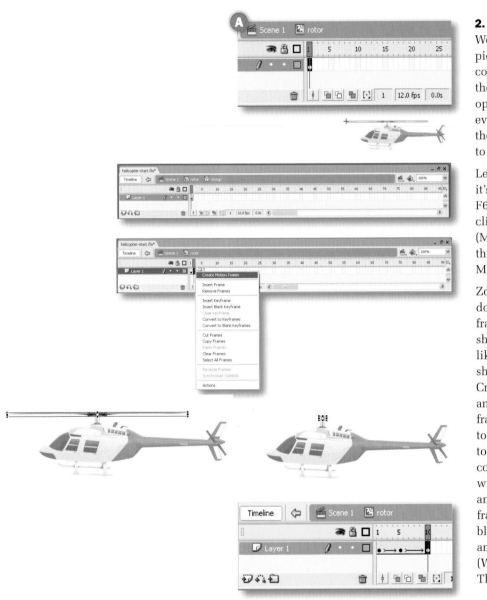

2. Animate the Nested Movie Clip

We'll start by animating the individual pieces before we move the entire helicopter across the stage. Double-click the rotor on the stage to edit it. Flash opens the rotor movie clip timeline, and everything but the rotor is dimmed on the stage **A**. Double-click the rotor again to open another timeline, called Group.

Let's make the rotor blade look like it's spinning. Select frame 5 and press F6 to create a keyframe. Then, right-click (Windows) or Control-click (Mac OS) one of the frames between the keyframes, and choose Create Motion Tween.

Zoom in so you can see what you're doing. Now, select the keyframe on frame 5. Use the Free Transform tool to shrink the roter blade so that it looks like it's facing us head-on. As the blade shrinks, it will appear to be rotating. Create another keyframe at frame 10, and another motion tween. Then select frame 10 and use the Free Transform tool to stretch the rotor blade back out to its original size; use the x in the corner as your guide. The animation will loop continuously. Because this is an intricate animation, let's change the frame rate from 12 fps to 24 fps. The blade will spin twice as fast. Test the animation so far by pressing Ctrl+Enter (Windows) or Cmd+Return (Mac OS). The blade appears to be spinning.

T I P

Bread Crumbs. Flash shows you which timeline is open, and the path to get there, at the top of the Timeline window. If you ever get confused about where you are, remember to look at the bread crumbs.

Dimensions:	775 px (width) x	400 px (height)
Match:	○ Printer ○ Contents ○ Default	
Background color:		
Frame rate:	24 fps	
Ruler units:	Pixels	

Make Default   OK   Cancel

3. Animate Other Nested Symbols

This helicopter has another moving part: the tail rotor. We'll animate it next. Return to Scene 1, the main stage. Though we dragged the tail rotor on as a single object, there are actually multiple pieces to it. We need to make it a single symbol. Double-click the tail rotor to open its timeline. Then, select

the whole blade and press F8. In the Convert to Symbol dialog box, select Graphic for the type and name the symbol Tail.

Now, select frame 6 and press F6 to create a keyframe. Right-click (Windows) or Control-click (Mac OS) any frame between the keyframes and choose Create Motion Tween. Flash is going to save us a bit of work here, with a rotation feature, so we don't have so spin this manually. Select the first keyframe. In the Properties Inspector, choose CW from the Rotate menu. Leave it set to rotate one time.

Return to Scene 1, and then press Ctrl+Enter (Windows) or Cmd+Return (Mac OS) to test it. The top rotor and tail rotor both spin, but not too elegantly. Increase the frame rate to 30 fps and shorten the tail rotor animation by a frame (press Shift+F5 to remove a frame). But that's not enough. We'll make it look smoother with a blur.

4. Add Filters for Effect

Return to Scene 1. Select the tail rotor. In the Filters panel, click the Plus button, and choose Blur. Selecting the right blur settings for a project can be a matter of trial and error. We'll use a setting of 2 for both the x and y values, and set the Quality to High.

Test it to see how the tail rotor looks now. The blur makes it look much smoother.

5. Animate the Main Object

The only thing left to do is to move the helicopter across the stage. Zoom out to 100% so you can see the full stage. We're working at 30 fps, a high frame rate. So let's create a keyframe at frame 70, a little over two seconds into the animation. Add a motion tween between the keyframes. Select frame 70, and move the helicopter to the upper-left corner of the stage.

Press Ctrl+Enter (Windows) or Cmd+Return (Mac OS) to test the movie. The helicopter flies across the stage, with its rotor blade and tail rotor spinning separately. ▦

Keyframes

Keyframes are frames that enable you to create changes across time.

About Keyframes

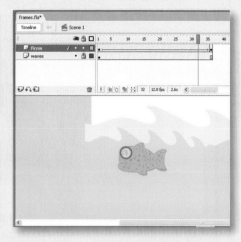

> ### TIP
>
> **Creating Keyframes.** To add frames to a layer when you need a keyframe, select the frame you want to add and press F6.

A frame is like a frame in a film. It contains an image that makes up part of your movie. A keyframe is a frame with additional properties. You use keyframes to mark the point at which an object's properties change for an animation, or to attach ActionScript. You can use keyframes to mark the beginning and end point of action and let frames tween the animation across the intermediate frames.

You can copy keyframes from one layer to another, move them, or delete them. Flash displays keyframes with a circle in the timeline. If the keyframe contains content, the circle is solid; if it is empty, the circle is empty. Frames that follow a keyframe have its content, until you insert another keyframe.

In later chapters, we'll label keyframes, attach ActionScript to them, use them to tween motion and shapes, copy them, delete them, and otherwise make them do our bidding.

Creating Keyframes

By default, the first frame in a Flash timeline is a keyframe. You can attach ActionScript to that first keyframe. However, if you need additional keyframes, you must insert them:

- Select a frame in the timeline and choose Insert > Timeline > Keyframe.

- Right-click (Windows) or Control-click (Mac OS) a frame in the timeline and choose Insert Keyframe.

- Select a frame in the timeline and press the F6 key.

Create a keyframe at the point that something changes, whether it's opacity, rotation, position, color, or shape. But don't create a keyframe for every frame. Flash includes the shapes on each keyframe in the final file, so the more content you have on keyframes, the larger the file size is going to be. For example, to make our friend Finnie move across the stage, we need just two keyframes and a motion tween. 🖽

Flash Detection

Add code to your movies to automatically detect the version of a viewer's Flash Player and help them download a later version, if necessary.

1. Specify the Player Version

Visitors to your website who don't have the latest version of the Flash Player installed may not be able to view your content. For example, a Flash 7 Player can't recognize new features in Flash 8, such as blending modes and filters. If you run a Flash 8 SWF in Player 7, the viewer will only see a white screen. Flash can include code in your movie to automatically detect a visitor's Flash Player version, and to route them to a download page if necessary.

Click on the screen outside the stage to change the settings for the entire document. In the Properties Inspector, click Settings next to Publish. In the Publish Settings dialog box, click the Flash tab. Choose the appropriate version number, such as Flash Player 8.

INSIGHT

Flash Player Version. If you choose Flash Player 8, Flash will prompt anyone using an earlier version of Flash Player to download the updated version. If you choose Flash Player 7, Flash will accept Flash Player 7 or 8. If your movie depends on Flash 8 features, choose Flash Player 8 so your viewers will see the movie, including filters, blending modes, and Vp6 video as you intended.

2. Include the HTML Code

Click the HTML tab. Select Detect Flash Version. When this option is selected, Flash writes the code into the HTML page to detect the viewer's version of Flash. If you want users to use a specific dot release of a Flash Player version, such as one that added new features or fixed issues, enter those numbers here.

By default, Flash publishes a Flash (SWF) file and an HTML file when you publish a movie. If you want to publish other formats, select them on the Formats tab of the Publish Settings dialog box. When you're ready to publish the movie, click Publish.

Flash creates the HTML page, with the detection code. When you open the HTML page, it loads the SWF file and the detection script. ▥

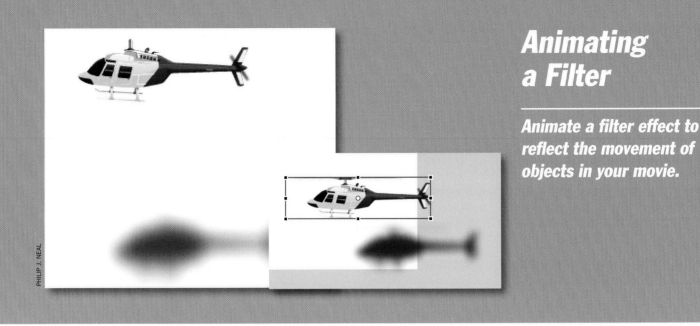

PHILIP J. NEAL

Animating a Filter

Animate a filter effect to reflect the movement of objects in your movie.

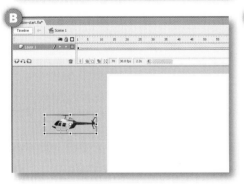

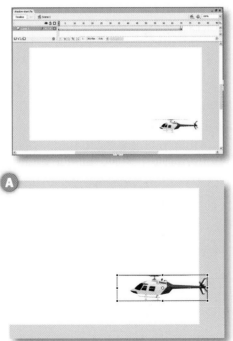

1. Animate the Object

We'll create a drop shadow for the helicopter we animated earlier, and to make it more realistic, we'll have the drop shadow move with the helicopter, getting larger as the helicopter flies higher. Open the file you used earlier, or the Shadow_start.fla file from the How to Wow CD.

Originally, we had the helicopter fly from the lower-right corner of the stage to the upper-left corner. Select the first keyframe, and then move the helicopter up a little from its starting point so there's more room for a shadow beneath it **A**. Let's also increase its size a little bit using the Free Transform tool, holding down the Shift key to keep it proportional.

Instead of just flying across the stage, let's have the helicopter fly right off the stage. Select the last keyframe. Move the helicopter off the stage. With the Free Transform tool, make the helicopter a little smaller and narrower, creating the impression that the helicopter is turning away from us as it flies away **B**.

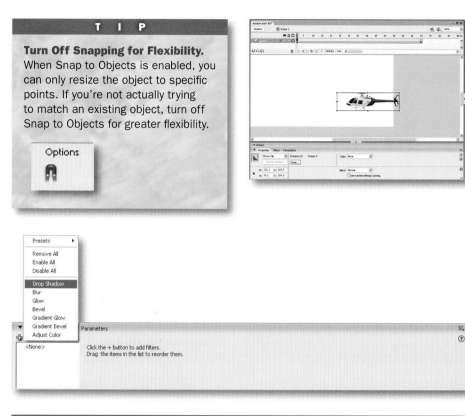

2. Create a Drop Shadow

We know what the object is going to do now, so we can add the drop shadow. Select the first keyframe. Select the helicopter, and open the Properties Inspector. The helicopter is a graphic symbol, so we can't apply a filter to it. Choose Movie Clip from the menu in the Properties Inspector to convert it; now we can apply filters to it.

Select the last keyframe and convert the instance to a movie clip symbol there as well.

Click the Filters tab. Then, click the Plus button and choose Drop Shadow.

The default drop shadow settings have the shadow too close to the helicopter. Experiment with Distance values to see what looks right on the screen; I'm going to use 130, so the shadow is just about at the bottom of the stage.

The edge of the shadow is too hard. Set the Blur to 17 for both x and y values, and choose Medium for Quality so a little bit of detail will show. And change Strength to about 80, for 80% opacity.

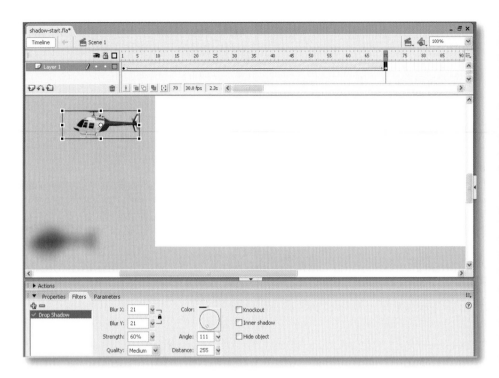

3. Animate the Drop Shadow

Currently, the drop shadow fades as the helicopter moves, because we haven't created a drop shadow for the last keyframe. Select that keyframe and change the settings in the Filters panel to change the blur to 21 for both the x and y values, reduce the strength to about 60%, and increase the distance to 255.

As an object moves, the angle of the shadow will also change. Think about where the sun would be and how it might cast a shadow. Click the Angle field and move the angle point to the appropriate location.

Test the movie by pressing Ctrl+Enter (Windows) or Cmd+Return (Mac OS). The helicopter takes off, with its rotor blade and tail rotor spinning separately, and its drop shadow moves with it. ▥

T I P

Increasing the Distance. The maximum distance for a drop shadow is 255, but if you want a shadow to be farther away, you can create an invisible object lower on the stage and create the drop shadow for it that matches the shadow of the object on screen. You can also use a higher setting if you employ ActionScript.

T I P

Testing the Movie. You can test a tween on the stage at anytime by choosing the first frame and pressing the Enter key on the keyboard. However, if you want to see any nested animations, you will need to press Ctrl+Enter (Windows) or Cmd+Return (Mac OS).

Making a DVD Project

Not all Flash movies are destined for the Web. You can publish yours to a CD-ROM or DVD for distribution, and set it up for full-screen display.

Self-Contained Flash Movie Files

PHILIP J. NEAL

Usually, when you publish a Flash movie, you create a SWF file. The viewer needs to have a version of Flash Player installed on the computer separately to view the movie. However, if you're distributing the movie on a CD-ROM or DVD, it's a good idea to create self-contained Flash movies called projectors.

We'll prepare a demonstration of how a firearm works, created by Philip Neal, for a CD-ROM. Click outside the stage to see the main document properties in the Properties Inspector. Click Settings next to Publish.

In the Publish Settings dialog box, select the Formats tab. Select Windows Projector and Macintosh Projector, and enter your desired name. Click Publish to publish the movie to these formats. Flash publishes the .exe and .hqx files. The .exe file will run the Flash movie if it's opened in Windows, and the .hqx file will run if it's opened in Mac OS. Burn all the files onto a CD or DVD, and distribute it. If you're going dual platform, it's more compatible to publish the projectors from a Macintosh computer.

Setting Screen Options

```
P12Fire-start.exe
P12Fire-start.fla
P12Fire-start.hqx
P12Fire-start.html
P12Fire-start.swf
```

```
1  fscommand("fullscreen", "true");
2  fscommand("allowscale", "true");
3  fscommand("showmenu", "false");
4
5
```

You can ensure that the movie always plays in full-screen mode using Action-Script. Let's set the P12fire_start.fla file to play in full-screen mode.

Select the first keyframe of the Actions layer, and open the Actions panel. Click Script Assist to enable it. Click Global Functions, then Browser/Network, and then double-click fsCommand to add it to the script. We need to select the appropriate options for this command. From the Commands for Standalone Player menu, choose fullscreen. There are two options there: true and false. True causes the movie to display in full screen, so that's what we want. You can add the fs command multiple times to use different options. For this project, we'd want allowscale to be true, so Flash will scale the images when it scales the window for full-screen display. We'd also choose showmenus and set it to false, so that menus won't appear.

When you have the settings you want, click Publish in the Publish Settings dialog box. Double-click the projector file to view it. Press Esc to quit a full-screen movie. Don't forget to copy the projector and all the assets to the CD. You can see an additional interface that has been created in the PhotoshopCAFE folder on the disk; this one plays videos.

2

CREATING IMAGERY

Using the powerful drawing tools in Flash

SINCE ITS INCEPTION, Flash has always been a drawing program. It began as SmartSketch, an application designed to help people draw on a computer. When its focus shifted to web-based animations, its name changed to FutureSplash. Macromedia saw its potential and turned it into the Flash that we all know and love today. Unless you have spent the last year or so on the moon, you know that Adobe Systems has now acquired Macromedia and we all hope for exciting integration between Adobe and Macromedia applications in the future.

No matter its name or which company owns it, and no matter how much developers are drawn to it for its support of ActionScript, Flash remains at its core about drawing and animation.

Flash includes some very powerful vector drawing tools. Many artists create all their artwork in Flash and go about their daily business without ever opening the Actions panel. Vectors are great because they're small in file size, easy to edit, and fully scalable. Of course, if you prefer, you can create artwork in Adobe Illustrator, Macromedia Freehand, Adobe Photoshop, or other applications, and then import it into Flash for animation. The software—and the techniques I'll show you—are flexible enough to adapt to your workflow.

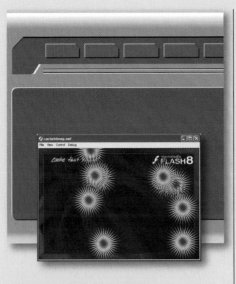

Filters and Blending Modes

Artists, designers, and animators have become very enthusiastic about new features in Flash 8. The professional version adds some very powerful tools to the creative arsenal.

Finally, filters are here. We can now create things like soft drop shadows, glows, and motion blurs easily. With earlier incarnations of Flash, we had to create two versions of artwork in an application such as Photoshop, one with the effect and one without; import both images into Flash; and then use tweens and alpha fades to generate effects. The new Flash filters not only make these effects easy to create but also drastically reduce the file size of Flash movies.

Likewise, blending modes make our lives much easier. For example, we no longer need to create transparency for some bitmap images to eliminate their black or white pixels; instead, just apply the Multiply or Overlay blending mode.

More Creative Options

With the new features in Flash 8, a whole new frontier of creative opportunity lies ready for us to explore.

In this chapter, I'll show you how to use some of the basic drawing tools in Flash to create artwork from scratch. We will make use of powerful drawing tools like gradients and learn the many ways that they can be manipulated. You'll meet a new friend, the object drawing model, and explore new ways of doing things. We will also be working with bitmap images in this chapter and combining them with vector images in some places. Throughout the course of this book, we'll take advantage of new features such as blending modes and filters. By the time you have finished reading and experimenting, it's my hope that you will be well equipped to go forward and create stunning content the likes of which no one has ever seen before.

COLIN SMITH

COLIN SMITH

Flash Drawing Models

The drawing model you use determines how objects interact with each other on the stage. Traditionally, Flash uses the Merge Drawing model, but Flash 8 also includes an alternative, the Object Drawing model.

Merge Drawing Model

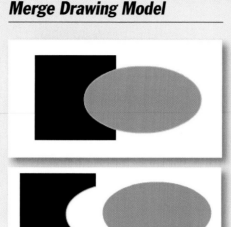

Object Drawing Model

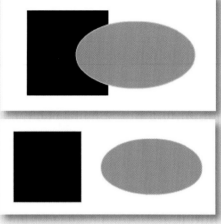

By default, Flash uses the Merge Drawing model. In this model, Flash merges overlapping drawn shapes, such as rectangles and ovals. If you move a shape that has been merged with another, the portion of the shape that was overlapping is permanently removed. You can take advantage of this drawing model to create customized shapes easily, as we will when we create a high-tech interface in the next lesson.

The Object Drawing model keeps drawn shapes distinct, so that they do not automatically merge or otherwise interact with other shapes on the stage. You can overlap shapes and then move them without changing the original shapes. In previous versions of Flash, you would have had to draw each shape on its own layer to keep it intact. When you select a shape created using the Object Drawing model, you'll see a rectangular bounding box. Use the Pointer tool to click the bounding box and drag the shape anywhere you'd like to position it.

To enable the Object Drawing model, select the Pencil, Line, Pen, Brush, Oval, Rectangle, or Polygon tool. Then, click the Object Drawing button in the Tools panel. 🎞

TIP

Converting a Shape. If you forgot to enable the Object Drawing model before drawing your shape, don't fret. You can convert the shape after it's drawn. Select it and then choose Modify > Combine Object > Union to convert the shape into a unified object. If you drew a shape with the Object Drawing model enabled, press Ctrl+B (Windows) or Cmd+B (Mac OS) to break it apart into pixels that behave as if they were created using the Merge Drawing model.

TIP

Quick Toggle. Press the J key to toggle between the Merge Drawing model and the Object Drawing model.

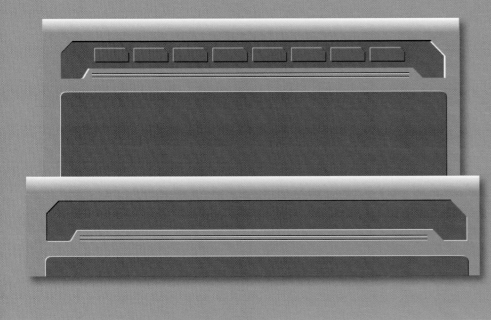

Design a High-Tech Interface

Use simple drawing techniques in Flash to create a high-tech look for a website. We will be using the new Object Drawing model in Flash 8.

1. Create a New Document

To create an interface for a website, let's start by defining an appropriate stage area. Open a new Flash document and then choose Modify > Document. Change the width of the document to 775 pixels, which is appropriate for today's monitors. Let's also select a background color that will let us see what we're doing easily; I'm using blue.

2. Create the Content Area

Let's create the area where most of the site's content will appear. We'll draw a rectangle with rounded corners.

Select the Rectangle tool **A** and make sure Object Drawing is enabled **B**. Select a gray fill and no stroke **D**, and then click the Set Corner Radius button in the Tools panel **C**. In the Rectangle Settings dialog box, specify a corner radius of 10 points **E**. Now draw a large rectangle like the one pictured.

3. Add Depth to the Content Area

To give the box some depth, we'll add a shadow and a highlight. In fact, we'll use a very simple method to do this: we'll make copies of the box in white and black, and then offset them slightly from the original.

Select the rectangle, and press Ctrl+C (Windows) or Cmd+C (Mac OS) to copy it. Then, choose Edit > Paste in Place or press Ctrl+Shift+V (Windows) or Cmd+Shift+V (Mac OS) to paste a copy in exactly the same position. Paste a second copy as well so that there are three versions stacked on top of each other.

Drag one of the rectangles off to the side to move it out of the way. Nudge the next one out of position so that you can select the bottom rectangle. Apply a fill of white to that copy. Then apply a fill of black to the second rectangle. Next, position the black rectangle directly on top of the white rectangle. Then press the right arrow key twice to nudge the black copy two pixels, and press the down arrow key twice to nudge the black rectangle two pixels down. Now, center the gray rectangle over the others; there should be single pixel of white along the top and left, and a single pixel of black along the bottom and right, creating the impression of depth.

Lock Layer 1 in the Timeline to ensure you don't accidentally make any changes to it.

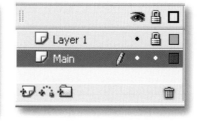

T I P

Zoom to Adjust Gradients.
You may have difficulty seeing the gradient angle when you adjust it, because the gradient boundaries are often larger than the stage. Zooming out to 50% lets you see the boundaries so you can adjust the gradient more efficiently.

4. Create the Background

Now we'll create a larger rectangle to serve as the main area of the interface. Create a new layer, name it Main, and move it beneath Layer 1 in the Timeline.

We'll draw a large gray rectangle, but this time with sharp corners. Select the Rectangle tool, and then click the Set Corner Radius button in the Tools panel. Change the corner radius to 0. Disable the Object Drawing so that we are drawing as a vector shape. Then, for the fill color, choose the black-to-white gradient. Now draw a rectangle that nearly fills the stage.

To modify the gradient, select the Gradient Transform tool from the tool panel and click the gradient on the stage. Then, click and drag the circle on the gradient boundary **A** to change the gradient angle. We'll spin this gradient so that the top is white and the bottom is black. Then, to make this gradient narrow, click the arrow **B** and move it toward the other boundary to change the gradient's width. Then, move that narrow gradient to the top of the rectangle by clicking and draging the gradient center point **C**.

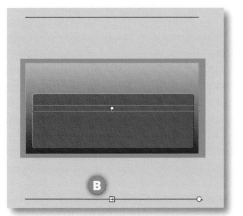

To soften the look, let's adjust the color of the gradient in the Color Mixer. (If it isn't already open, choose Window> Color Mixer.) Because a gradient is selected, the Color Mixer displays a gradient bar with white at one end and black at the other. Double-click the black icon, and then choose a light gray from the color picker. The background is in great shape. Lock the Main layer to ensure you don't accidentally make any changes to it.

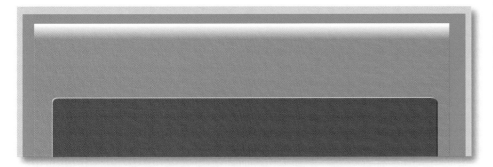

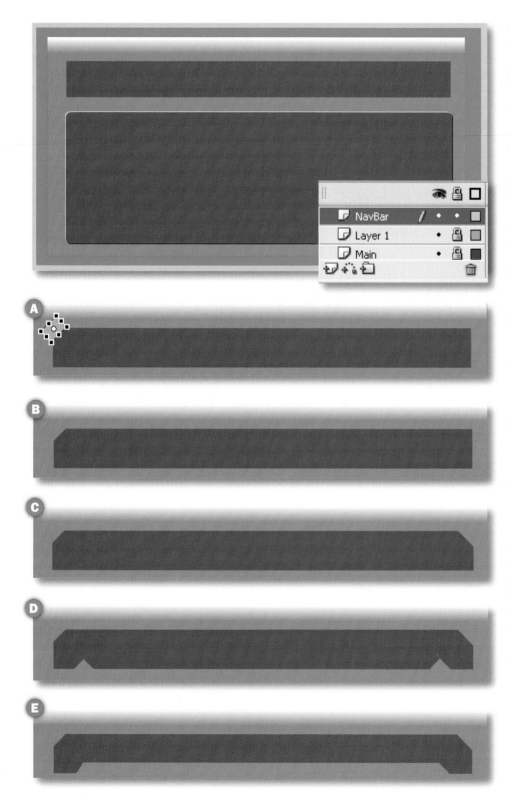

5. Create the Navigation Bar

Every website needs a navigation bar so that visitors can find their way around. Start by creating a new layer, named NavBar, and then move it to the first position in the Timeline.

Once again, select the Rectangle tool, and make sure the Object Drawing model is off. We'll use the same color we used in the content area, so unlock Layer 1, and then use the Eyedropper tool to pick up that color. Then, draw a rectangle above the content area.

For a sharp, high-tech effect, we'll cut out the corners on the navigation bar. This is where the Merge Drawing model makes a difference. Draw a small rectangle in any color. Use the Free Transform tool to rotate it and position it on the corner of the navigation bar so that it cuts across a 45-degree angle **A**.

Click away and then reselect and move the small rectangle. Flash removes the area that overlapped **B**. Do the same with the other corner **C**.

Use the same technique to remove a section of the navigation bar. First, turn off Snap to Objects so that you can place the rectangle where you want it: select the rotated rectangle, and choose View > Snapping > Snap to Objects. Then, place the rectangle where you want a cut-out, click away to deselect, reselect the rectangle and move the rectangle revealing the cutout **D**. Repeat this process to make a second notch at the other end of the navigation bar. For this interface, we'll also remove the area between two cutouts. To do this, choose the selection tool and then carefully make a rectangular selection between the two triangles. Once selected, press Delete **E**.

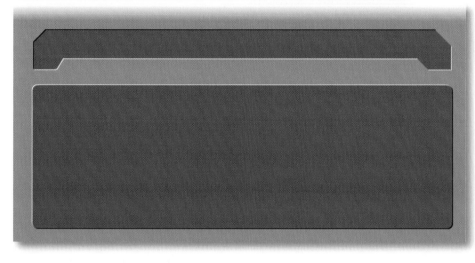

6. Add Depth to the Nav Bar

We'll add depth to the navigation bar using a slightly different technique than we used before. This time, let's convert the object to a symbol. Select the navigation bar, and then choose Modify > Convert to Symbol, or press F8. In the Convert to Symbol dialog box, select Graphic for the type, and name the symbol Nav.

As we did before, we'll make a couple of copies. So press Ctrl+C (Windows) or Cmd+C (Mac OS) to copy the symbol, and then press Ctrl+Shift+V (Windows) or Cmd+Shift+V (Mac OS) twice to paste two copies. Move one of the copies out of the way, and move another slightly to the side. To make the navigation bar appear to be inset, we'll reverse the shadow and highlight positions, by placing the shadow to the left and up one pixel. We will nudge the highlight down one pixel and to the right.

We can't change the color of a symbol without affecting the other two instances, so we need to break the symbol apart: select the bottom symbol and press Ctrl+B (Windows) or Cmd+B (Mac OS) to break it. Now, apply a black fill to it. Then align the next symbol on top of the black copy, and nudge it two pixels down and two pixels to the right. Press Ctrl+B (Windows) or Cmd+B (Mac OS) to break it apart, and then apply a white fill to it. Now move the top symbol, which can remain gray, into position so that a single line of white pixels shows at the bottom and right, and a single line of black pixels shows at the top and left.

T I P

Precise Placement. To ensure that you're positioning objects accurately in Flash, use ruler guides. Choose View > Rulers, and then drag a vertical guide from the side ruler or a horizontal guide from the top ruler. The guides won't appear in the movie, but they can help you keep things orderly.

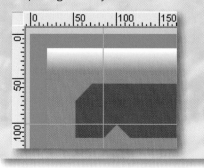

I N S I G H T

Organizing Files. You can quickly accumulate a large number of layers in a Flash project. To keep those layers organized, take advantage of layer folders. Here, we've created a folder called Interface to hold the layers we've created so far. Then, as we add other types of layers, we can create separate folders for them. It's much easier to open a folder to see the layers in it than to have to scroll through dozens of layers.

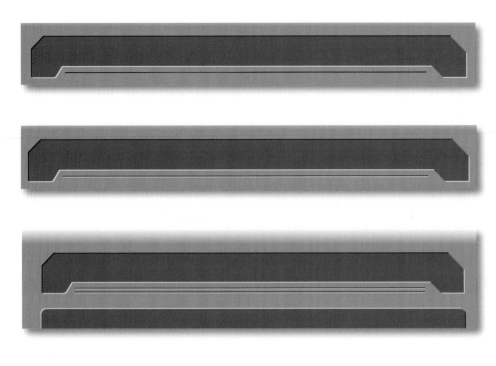

7. Add Inset Lines

Let's add some etched lines, tucked into the space under the navigation bar. First, create a new layer and call it Lines. Then, set the stroke color to black, and use the Line tool to draw a line. Hold down the Shift key as you draw to constrain the line. To give the line depth, copy it and paste it in place once. Nudge the copy down a pixel, and change its color to white. Presto! We have an inset line.

It'd be nice to have a second etched line. To copy it easily, first convert it into a symbol. Select both lines—use the Shift key to select multiple objects—and press F8. In the Convert to Symbol dialog box, select Graphic for type and name the symbol Lines. To duplicate the symbol, just press the Alt (Windows) or Option (Mac OS) key while you drag out a copy.

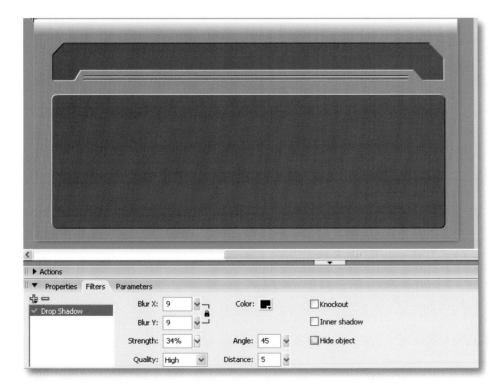

8. Add a Drop Shadow

Let's add more depth to the interface by giving the background a drop shadow. Unlock the Main layer, which contains the background. Effects, including the drop shadow effect, can only be applied to symbols, so we'll need to convert the background to a symbol: Select the background and press F8. In the Convert to Symbol dialog box, select Movie Clip for the type, and name the symbol Background.

To add a drop shadow, open the Filters panel (with the background symbol selected), click the Plus icon, and choose Drop Shadow. Let's increase the blur to 8 or 9 and decrease the strength to about 34% to lighten the shadow. Set the Quality to High. That gives us a nice, subtle drop shadow for an elegant look.

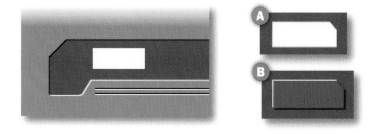

9. Create Buttons

Our interface needs buttons, so let's add some to the navigation bar. Create a new layer called Button. Then, use the Rectangle tool with the Object Drawing model off, with no stroke and a white fill, to draw a small rectangular button. Then, using the technique we used to customize the navigation bar, use a small square to clip the corner off the button **A**.

To give the button some depth, copy it and then paste it into place once. Use arrow keys to nudge that copy two pixels down and two pixels to the right. Fill it with black. Then paste another copy, center it over the others, and fill it with a button color **B**. I've used a nice dark green.

Convert the whole thing to a symbol. Select all three layers by drawing a marquee around them with the Selection tool. Then press F8. In the Convert to Symbol dialog box, select Button for the type and name the symbol Button.

Duplicate the button by holding down the Alt (Windows) or Option (Mac OS) key and dragging copies to the side. When you have all the buttons you need, quickly align them using the Align panel. Distribute the centers horizontally and align the top edges.

To get a better view while working we set the stage color to blue. For a more appealing setting for the final interface, change the background to a light gray or other unobtrusive color. ▥

Runtime Bitmap Caching

Flash 8 includes a bitmap caching feature, which enables you to play back very complex animated vector graphics without sacrificing the quality of the movie's performance.

About Bitmaps

Bitmaps, also called rasters, define every pixel in an object. Bitmaps are useful for complex photographs or interface elements where data changes subtly from one pixel to another. However, because they contain so much data, bitmap graphics usually have larger file sizes than vector graphics, and they take longer to download. Additionally, the quality of a bitmap graphic is directly dependent on its resolution; if you resize a bitmap graphic or display it at a different resolution, the quality suffers.

You've worked with bitmap data if you've edited photographs in Photoshop or other photo-editing software. There are ways to compress the data to reduce a graphic's file size, but you may compromise quality. However, because they include all the data, bitmap movies display smoothly.

COLIN SMITH

About Vectors

Vector art is a mathematical representation of lines, curves, color, and position. Vectors offer many advantages over bitmaps, especially for website design. For example, vector art requires less information, resulting in smaller file sizes and faster download times than comparable bitmap images. Additionally, vectors are resolution-independent, so you can scale it or display it any resolution without losing clarity.

You've probably created vector objects if you've worked in FreeHand, Illustrator, or other drawing applications. In Flash, you create vector objects in much the same way, although there are a few tools that are unique to Flash.

If a Flash movie contains complex vector artwork, it may appear jerky because Flash needs to constantly redraw the vector elements. It's difficult to show this behavior on the printed page, but you can easily see it for yourself using the sample file that comes with Flash 8. Navigate to Flash 8/Samples and Tutorials/ActionScript/CacheBitmap on your hard drive. Open the Cachebitmap.fla file and then press Ctrl+Enter (Windows) or Cmd+Enter (Mac OS) to preview the movie. The vector objects do not move smoothly.

CHRIS GEORGENES

Bitmap Caching

Runtime bitmap caching gives you the best of both worlds: the small file size of vectors with the smooth playback of bitmaps. You can specify that a static movie clip or button symbol be cached as a bitmap at the time the movie is run, preventing Flash from having to continually redraw the symbol. Bitmap caching lets you "freeze" a movie clip in place automatically, and Flash uses vector data to update the bitmap cache if anything changes. This minimizes the number of redraws that Flash Player must perform, and provides smoother, faster playback performance.

For example, if you're creating an animation with a complex background, you can create a movie clip for the background, rendered as a bitmap stored at the current screen depth. It can be drawn quickly, and doesn't need to be continually redrawn, so the animation plays faster and more smoothly.

Runtime bitmap caching is ideal for complex movie clips where the position of the objects changes, but not when the shape or content of the objects changes. Don't use runtime bitmap caching when objects change size, shape or color, for example, or when you're working with simple movie clips. Bitmap caching also works very well in cases where you have a number of vectors all animated on the stage at the same time.

To specify bitmap caching, select the movie clip or button symbol on the stage, and then select Use Runtime Bitmap Caching in the Property Inspector. An additional purpose for bitmap caching

is creating masks with different levels of transparency. You can only apply these masks with ActionScript and bitmap caching must be enabled on both the mask and the object that your masking. In Chapter 4, you will learn how to create these masks that use alpha channels.

Create a Button to Perform a Simple Action

Design a three-dimensional button to move an object across the stage and stop it there.

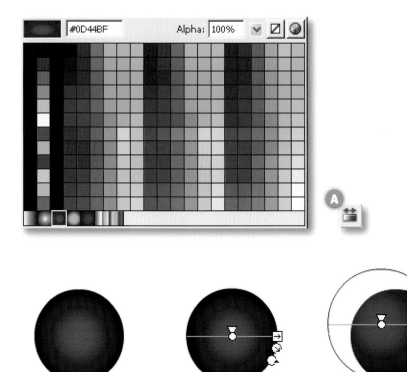

1. Create the Button Shape

We'll create a button that moves an airplane across the stage. You could draw your own plane if you wanted to, but we've provided one for you to use. Open button_start.fla to get started.

First, draw a circle. Select the Oval tool, and set it to have no stroke and a red gradient fill. Hold down the Shift key as you draw to constrain the oval to a perfect circle. By default, the gradient starts from the center, so it appears that light is hitting the circle from above. For a more realistic three-dimensional effect, we'll modify the gradient. Select the Gradient Transform tool **A**, and click on the circle. The Gradient Transform tool provides several options. Click the circle in the center and drag the lighting source to the upper-left corner; pull the arrows out to increase the size of the lit area. You can adjust the gradient to get just the look you want.

2. Convert the Shape to a Button

Select the circle with the Selection tool, and choose Modify > Convert to Symbol. In the Convert to Symbol dialog box, name the symbol Button, select Button for the type, and leave the registration point in the upper-left corner. The registration point determines the point from which transformation or positioning is done. It's easier to predict your results if you leave the registration point in the upper-left corner. Click OK. The button appears in the library.

3. Define the Rollover States

It's customary for a button to have different appearances to indicate that it's been selected or to show that the pointer has rolled over it. We'll define the button's appearance for different rollover states. Double-click the button on the stage or in the library. Rollover states appear in the Timeline: Up, Over, Down, and Hit.

First, we'll quickly give each state the same content as the Up, or default, state. Hold Alt (Windows) or Option (Mac OS) and drag the dot under the Up state to the Over state. The square in the Timeline appears filled. Do the same thing for each of the other states. This defines all the states identically, and ensures that the Hit state is the exact size of the button.

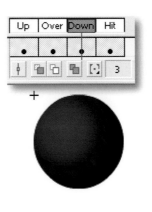

Next, change the Over state so that the button appears green when you move the mouse over it. Select the Over state in the Timeline, and then select a green gradient fill in the Tools panel.

Let's change the Down state to blue. Select the Down state, and then apply the blue gradient fill.

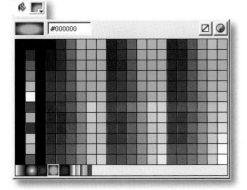

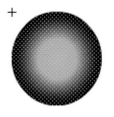

To test the button states, return to Scene 1. Then choose Control > Enable Simple Buttons. This command makes buttons on stage behave as they will in the final movie. Move the mouse over the button; it should turn green. When you click the button, it should turn blue. When you've tested the button, choose Control > Enable Simple Buttons again to return to edit mode.

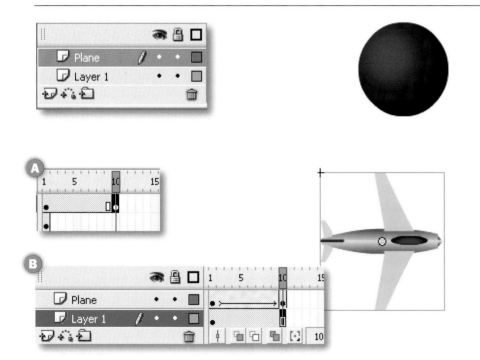

4. Add a Moving Object

Create a new layer and name it Plane. Then, click on the first frame, a keyframe, in the Timeline. Drag the plane symbol from the library onto the left side of the stage.

To make the plane move across the stage, we'll create a simple motion tween. Select frame 10 and press the F6 key to insert a keyframe **A**. Flash creates a solid circle on the frame to show that it's a keyframe. Now click on the airplane, hold down the Shift key (to constrain a horizontal movement), and drag the plane to the other side of the stage.

Next, right-click between the first and tenth frames, and choose Create Motion Tween. If you scrub through the Timeline, the plane moves steadily from one side of the stage to the other. However, after you move past the first frame, the button disappears. To ensure the button stays visible the entire time, click on frame 10 for Layer 1 (the layer the button is on) and then choose Insert > Timeline > Frame to copy the contents of the first frame through nine more frames **B**. You could alternatively press F5 to create a frame.

5. Prevent the Object from Moving Automatically

Currently, the plane moves across the stage when you play the movie. But we want the plane to stay in position until the button is pressed. To accomplish this, we need to add an action. First, create a separate layer for actions, and move it to the top of the Layers palette. Next, select the first frame, and then open the Actions panel at the bottom of the screen.

This is a very simple action, so we're not going to use Script Assist. If it's enabled in your application, just click it to disable it. Then, type

```
stop ();
```

This action stops the movie when it gets to the first frame, so that the plane doesn't move.

6. Add an Action to the Button

Now we need to add an action to the button so that pressing it causes the plane to move. Select the button, and then open the Actions panel again. Its heading should say Actions-Button. And this time, click Script Assist to enable it. Click the Plus symbol **A** and then choose Global Functions > Movie Clip Control > On. Flash provides several options here.

INSIGHT

About Motion Tweens. When you need to move an object from one position to another over time, a motion tween can save you tedious steps. The term tween is short for in between. To define a motion tween animation, define the starting and ending positions for the object, and then let Flash calculate all of the intermediate positions for the object.

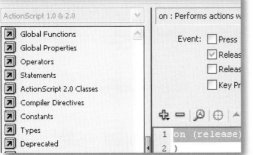

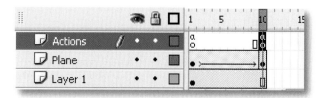

```
1  on (release) {
2      gotoAndPlay(2);
3  }
4
```

We'll keep Release selected so that the action happens when we release the mouse.

We want Flash to go to frame 2 when the mouse is released. Click at the end of line 1 in the script, and then press the + symbol again and choose Global Functions > Timeline Control > Goto. By default, Flash has added Goto and Play, which is appropriate for this button. However, we need to change the frame number to 2.

That's all we need. Once we release the mouse, it will go to and play frame 2. Close the Actions panel. To test the movie, press Ctrl+Enter (Windows) or Cmd+Enter (Mac OS). Click the button to see the plane move.

7. Add a Keyframe to Stop the Object

By default, Flash loops movies, so when the movie is finished, the plane returns to its initial position, but it won't move again until the button is pressed. To keep the plane from returning to its initial position, we need to add a keyframe. Click on frame 10 and choose Insert > Timeline > Keyframe or press F6. replace with TIF Now open the Actions panel, and type

```
stop ();
```

Now when we press the button, the plane moves across the stage and stops. ▥

COLIN SMITH

Create Image Thumbnails

Display your favorite images as thumbnails, which interact with the mouse.

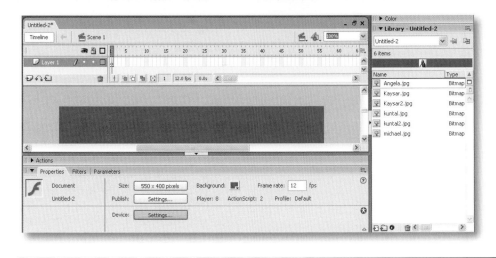

1. Import the Images to the Library

Before you can create thumbnails of images in Flash, you need to add them to the library. First, create a new Flash document. I've set the background to a dark gray so it's easier to see what we're doing with white shapes.

Then, choose File > Import > Import to Library. Select the images you want to import (Shift-click to select more than one), and click Open. Flash adds the images to the library, but doesn't place them on the stage.

2. Create the Thumbnail Shape

You can create a thumbnail in any shape. We'll create a rectangular shape with an angular cut in the corner. First, rename the layer Thumbnail. Select the Rectangle tool in the toolbox. Make sure both Object Drawing and Snap to Objects are disabled, and set the stroke to none and the fill to white. Then, draw a small rectangle.

T I P

Resize to Optimize. If you're not going to need a full-size image, resize JPEG images to the approximate size you'll need before importing them into your Flash file. You can resize images in a photo-editing application, such as Adobe Photoshop.

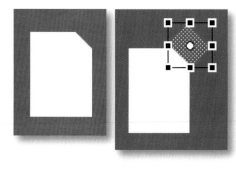

To create the angular cut, draw a small square in a different color. Then, select the Free Transform tool, and press the Shift key as you rotate the rectangle to a 45-degree angle. Drag the rectangle to the corner, click elsewhere on the page, and delete the small rectangle. Flash removes the overlapping area from the original rectangle.

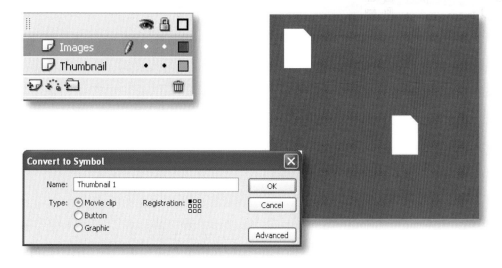

3. Create a Thumbnail Symbol

To keep things tidy, create a new layer and name it Images.

We'll create a copy of the shape to use for the first thumbnail: select the thumbnail, and choose Edit > Copy. Then, lock the Thumbnail layer, and select the Images layer. Now, choose Edit > Paste In Center. A copy of the shape appears in the center of the stage.

Next, we'll convert the shape to a symbol. Select the shape you just pasted, and press F8. In the Convert to Symbol dialog box, select Movie Clip, name it Thumbnail 1, and click OK. The symbol appears in the library.

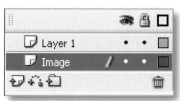

4. Fill the Thumbnail with an Image

Let's add an image to the thumbnail symbol. Double-click the thumbnail in the library or on the stage to edit it. Notice that in the Navigator, we've moved from Scene 1, the main stage, to Thumbnail 1 **A**, because that's what we're working in right now.

Create another layer for images and name it, appropriately, Image. Drag the Image layer beneath Layer 1.

Drag an image from the library onto the stage. It's the full-size image. We need to resize it for the thumbnail.

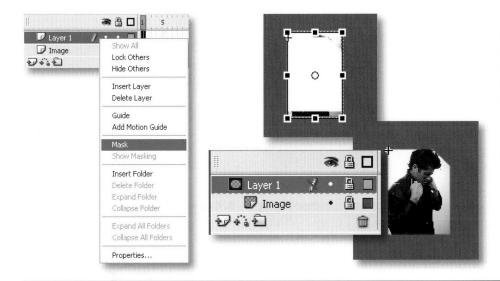

Holding down the Shift key to keep the image proportional, use the Free Transform tool to resize the image to approximately the size of the thumbnail. The area that will appear in the thumbnail is the area currently hidden by its shape.

Right-click Layer 1 and choose Mask. The image layer is nested under Layer 1 in the Layers palette.

Lock the Image layer to see the masked thumbnail; only the part of the image that overlapped the original shape shows.

5. Create Additional Thumbnails

To keep the stage neat, return to Scene 1, and then drag the thumbnail to the upper-left corner of the stage. Now, let's create thumbnails for the other images in the library.

To duplicate the thumbnail, press Alt+Shift (Windows) or Option+Shift (Mac OS) and drag the thumbnail to the right. Release the mouse, and there's the copy. Duplicate the thumbnail as many times as you need to for the number of images you're using. I have four images, so I've made four copies.

6. Replace Images in Duplicate Thumbnails

The thumbnails are all displaying the same image, because they're instances of the same symbol. To replace the images in individual thumbnails, we'll need to duplicate the symbol. First, unlock the Thumbnail layer. Then right-click the second thumbnail and choose Duplicate Symbol. Name the symbol Thumbnail 2. Name the other symbols Thumbnail 3 and Thumbnail 4. The symbols appear in the library.

To replace the image for a thumbnail, double-click it, unlock the Image layer, and then right-click the thumbnail. Choose Swap Bitmap. Select the replacement image, and click OK. Flash automatically uses the cropping information from the original image. You may need to adjust the image for the thumbnail size a little, as we will with Angela's picture.

Click the Free Transform tool, press Shift, and resize. When you're satisfied with it, lock the layer so you can see the mask. Replace the images in the other thumbnails the same way.

7. The Invisible Button Trick

Because we want to use these thumbnails as buttons, we'll define rollover states for each of them. Let's start by converting the initial thumbnail shape to a button. Return to Scene 1, unlock the Thumbnail layer, and drag it above the Images layer.

Then, drag the thumbnail shape on top of the first thumbnail image. You can turn on Snap to Object to ensure the thumbnail shape is directly on top of the first thumbnail.

With the thumbnail shape selected, press F8. In the Convert to Symbol dialog box, select Button for the symbol type and name it Button.

Press Alt+Shift and drag the button to each of the other thumbnails to create three copies. Each of these buttons is an instance of the same symbol, so updating one will update them all.

Double-click on a button. We'll create four different states: Up, Over, Down, and Hit. To start, copy the Up state's contents to the others: press Alt or Option and drag to each state.

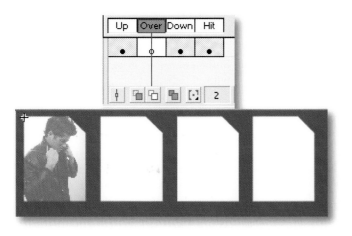

In the Over state, we want the image to appear in full color: select the Over state in the Timeline and press Delete or Backspace to reveal the image. In the Down state, we want the white box to appear, so we'll leave that unchanged. In the Up, or default, state, we want the image to be dimmed, so we'll need to change the transparency of the shape. To change the alpha, we first need to convert the shape to a symbol, so press F8, select Movie Clip for the type, and name it Alpha Thumbnail. In the Properties palette, select Alpha for the color and change the opacity to about 40%. We'll change our background back to white for final presentation.

Test your rollovers by pressing Ctrl+Enter (Windows) or Cmd+Enter (Mac OS). The thumbnails are all dimmed by default; as you roll over an image, you see it more clearly. When you click on an image, it turns white. This makes it obvious to the user that something is happening when they interact with the gallery.

This concludes setting up the thumbnails. To add interactivity to these and finish the gallery, check out Chapter 6.

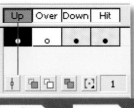

INSIGHT

Different Timelines and Layers.
The layers we created earlier were part of Scene 1. When you double-click the thumbnail symbol, the layers in the Timeline change to reflect the object that we're editing. When we add a layer now, we're adding it to the Timeline for the thumbnail object, not to Scene 1.

COLIN SMITH

Scanlines and Patterns

Use simple patterns to add texture effects to your Flash creations.

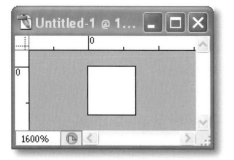

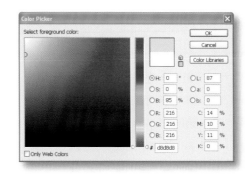

1. Create the Pattern in Photoshop

We'll start by creating a basic pattern in Adobe Photoshop. If you don't have Photoshop, you can use the patterns included on the How to Wow CD. But if you do have Photoshop, you can get as creative as you want in designing your own patterns.

First, open a new document in Photoshop. For a basic diagonal pattern, we'll use a canvas size of 3 pixels by 3 pixels. Then zoom in to 1600% so that each pixel is large and easy to work with. We'll create a pattern using color. You can choose the foreground color you want to use from the color picker.

I've chosen a light gray. To fill the entire canvas with the color, press Alt+Backspace (Windows) or Option+Delete (Mac OS). Now let's paint with a darker gray; select a dark gray from the color picker.

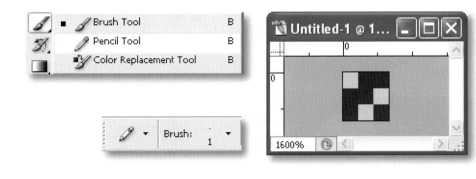

Next, select the Pencil tool; you may have to click the Brush tool to see it. Make sure the pencil diameter is set to 1 pixel. Click diagonally across the square, and add a couple more pixels to create a ricrac effect. This is the pattern you'll use to create the texture in Flash. Choose File > Save For Web or Save As, and save the file as a PNG file named Diagonal.png. Select None in the PNG Options dialog box when it appears.

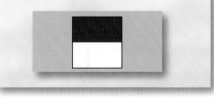

2. Apply the Pattern in Flash

In Flash, open the file you want to add texture to. I'm using the Patterns.fla file off the How to Wow CD.

Create a layer for the pattern. In this file, we'll position the layer between the interface and background layers, because we want the texture to appear above the background but behind the top interface.

Next, create a rectangle the appropriate size for the texture. Select the Rectangle tool, and make sure there's no stroke. You can use any fill color. If you're working with Patterns.fla, draw a rectangle the size of the box the car is in.

Now we'll replace that fill with the pattern. In the Color Mixer, choose Bitmap from the Type menu. (If the Color Mixer isn't open, choose Window > Color Mixer.) Click Import, and select the patterns you want to use. Now, make sure the Pattern layer is selected, and choose Bitmap in the Color Mixer again, and then select the pattern you want to use. Flash tiles the pattern seamlessly across the rectangle.

3. Blend the Pattern with the Background

We don't want to cover up everything else; we want to blend the texture in. We'll need to use blending modes, and only movie clip symbols support blending modes. So, with the rectangle selected, press F8. In the Convert to Symbol dialog box, select Movie Clip for the type, and name it rpattern, for repeating pattern.

Now, open the Properties Inspector, and experiment with blending modes. Lighten is an interesting effect. Overlay is subtle and sophisticated. To make it subtler, adjust the alpha value to 40%.

T I P

Alpha Equals Opacity. If you're used to using other Adobe applications, think of the Alpha value as the Opacity value. The higher the value, the greater the opacity; the lower the value, the greater the transparency.

I N S I G H T

Changing Patterns. If you want to try different patterns with your image, you needn't re-create the symbol. Just double-click the pattern, and then click the Fill icon again in the Color Mixer, choose Bitmap, select a new bitmap pattern, and return to the scene. Different patterns can create

strikingly different results. Here's the same image with a scanline pattern, using Overlay blending mode and an alpha value of 40%.

Repurpose an Animated GIF

Easily convert an animated GIF file to a Flash movie.

1. Import the GIF File into a New Document

You can import an animated GIF file into Flash without making any changes to it. Flash will recognize the GIF as an animation and create a new keyframe for each of the frames in the animation. It will also place each of the frames into the library as a separate image.

First, create a new Flash document that is the size of the GIF file you're importing. I'm using a banner ad, which is 600 pixels by 100 pixels. We'll keep the frame rate and the background color the same.

Then, choose File > Import to Stage, select the GIF file, and click Open. Flash automatically adds each of the frames from the animation to your document. It brings each frame into the document as a separate bitmap, which is included in the library.

2. Export the Movie

You can make changes to the animation if you choose to. There may be some tweens that can be created more efficiently in Flash, or perhaps replace the text with nice crisp vector text. To export the movie, choose File > Export > Export Movie. Name the movie and specify a location for it. Then, change the settings in the Export Flash Player dialog box, where you can specify which version of Flash Player the movie supports.

If you choose to, you can also optimize each image in the animation to bring the file size down further. Flash produces much smoother animations at a fraction of the file size of a GIF.

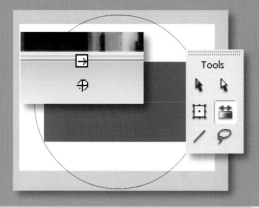

Transform Gradients

You can adjust the direction, size, or center of a gradient fill using the Gradient Transform tool. First, create the gradient. Then, select the Gradient Transform tool, and click the area that contains the gradient. Flash displays a bounding box with editing handles. The pointer icon changes as you roll over gradient handles.

Center point

The pointer icon for the center point handle is a four-way arrow. Select and drag this handle to move the gradient's center point.

Focal point

The focal point is the point from which the gradient radiates, so it's only available for a radial gradient. The pointer icon for the focal point handle is an inverted triangle; click and drag this handle to shift the focal point.

Size

The pointer icon for the size handle is a shape with an arrow in it. Click and drag this handle on the edge of the bounding box to change the gradient's size. Resizing the gradient changes only the gradient itself, not the size of the object containing it.

Rotation

The pointer icon for the rotation handle is four arrows in the shape of a circle for the radial gradient, and a circle with a triangle on the linear gradient. Click and drag the bottom handle on the edge of the bounding box to change the gradient's rotation. Press the Shift key to constrain the direction of a linear gradient fill to multiples of 45-degrees.

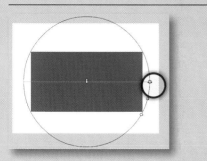

Width

The pointer icon for the width handle is a double-ended arrow on the radial gradient. Click and drag the square handle to adjust the width of the gradient. ▥

3

ALIVE WITH MOTION

Use motion in creative ways to add interest and pizazz to your projects.

SLIDE IN WITH MOTION BLUR 60

ANIMATED PAGE TRANSITIONS 64

LOGO SHEEN 67

SHIMMERING METAL 70

FREEHAND WRITING 74

MOTION ON A PATH 76

UNROLLING A SCROLL 79

MASKING 83

ANIMATION IS THE HOOK that brings most of us to Flash. If you're holding this book in your hands, you probably have a keen interest, perhaps even a fascination, with animation. The word animate means "bring to life." And that's just what we'll do in this chapter: bring static web pages and multimedia projects to life.

We are not just going to make things move. We are going to make things move in new and cool ways. I'm sure you have seen the movie websites where things slide in, shimmer, gleam, and unroll right before your eyes. I'll show you how to create these types of effects for yourself. You'll notice once you get into this chapter that a lot of these effects are not as difficult as they look. Everything is an illusion. I get a kick out of watching the creative ways people are using Flash. The hardest part is getting people to share their secrets, which I do openly in this book. I wish that I had had these pages to read years ago!

We'll combine filters with motion to create some really useful effects. We'll animate masks, which bring tremendous possibilities to your projects. We'll create page transitions that will open eyes and get attention. I encourage you to follow along, learn these techniques, and then adapt them so that you can inject your very own creative touch to your work.

A quick word of warning: It's easy to abuse these effects just as people have abused animated GIFs. It used to be all the rage to create long animated introductions for every Flash site, but today it's known as "Flashturbation." Use these effects wisely and your visitors will love you, but abuse them and you may receive some nasty glances from across the Web. The key is to use effects with taste and moderation. Just because you can do something doesn't mean you that you should. Usability is very important. Effects should not hinder the visitor's browsing experience; they should enhance it. I find it's best to avoid animated intros and just have some animation on the

page as the site builds. Nice animations for transitions and some tasteful effects will go a long way.

In this chapter, I'll show you how to mimic some real-world effects, such as light reflecting off metal, an invisible hand writing across the screen, a sheet of paper unrolling to reveal an image, and a fish named "Finnie" jumping out of the water. Why are you still reading this? Let's get started!

COLIN SMITH

COLIN SMITH

Slide-In with Motion Blur

What do you get when you combine a motion tween, blur, and transparency? The cool effect you see on movie websites, where the image races in and stops with elegance.

1. Turn the Graphic into a Movie Clip Symbol

I'm using the Slidein_start.fla file, available on your How to Wow CD. There are already several layers in the file—an Actions layer that contains a Stop action to keep the movie from looping, a Nav_text layer, a Person layer for the fellow we'll be sliding in, a Background layer, and the Feet layer that I'll talk about more later. Hide the Feet layer for now.

Drag the Kaysar-web_Curves 1.png file from the library onto the stage. I created this file in Photoshop from one of my photo shoots.

Drag the object into its final position. (You'll see the bounding box match the stage size.) We'll convert it to a movie clip symbol so we can animate it. Press F8, select Movie Clip for the type, and name it Kaysar.

2. Create a Motion Tween

The person is in the final position, but that's not where we want him to start. Select frame 14, and press F6 to create a keyframe. Now we can create a motion tween between frame 1, which is automatically a keyframe, and the keyframe we just created.

Right-click the timeline between the keyframes, and choose Motion Tween. Now, move to frame 1, and then position the movie clip where we want it to be at the beginning, with the person just off the stage to the right. Because we've created the tween, Flash moves the person from the beginning position to the end position as we scrub through the timeline.

When we get to frame 15, Kaysar disappears because we've run out of frames on that layer. To quickly duplicate the last frame, click frame 60 and press F5. Flash fills in the additional frames with the content of frame 14.

To test the movie, press Ctrl+Enter (Windows) or Cmd+Enter (Mac OS). Kaysar slides in and then stays in position.

TIP

Two Ways To Tween. You can right-click the Timeline between the keyframes, as we did here, or click the timeline and choose Motion from the Tween menu in the Properties Inspector.

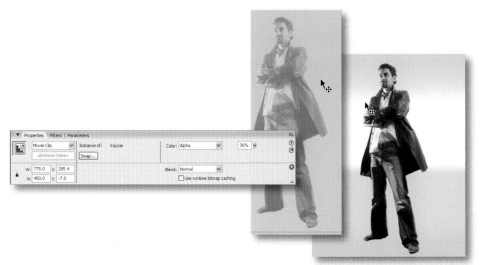

3. Adjust the Opacity

Let's have Kaysar be nearly transparent at the start, and gradually increase the opacity until he's fully opaque. Select the first frame and open the Properties Inspector. Click on the movie clip. Choose Alpha from the Color option in the Properties Inspector, and lower the alpha to 36%. Now the beginning frame shows Kaysar to the right of the stage and 36% opaque, and the last frame shows him in the final position and 100% opaque. Flash tweens the opacity just as it tweens the motion. To see the effect, press Ctrl+Enter (Windows) or Cmd+Enter (Mac OS).

4. Add Motion Blur

We also want to create a motion blur effect, and we can do that using a filter. In fact, in Flash 8, we can tween filters and effects, which gives us many more possibilities. Select frame 1. Select the movie clip again, and open the Filters panel. Click the Plus sign, and choose Blur. The x value is the horizontal blur and the y value is the vertical blur. By default, the x and y values are linked, so when you increase one, you increase both. We want to increase only the horizontal blur, so click the padlock icon to separate the values. Set the y value to 0 and increase the x value to 24. As we move through the timeline, the person moves from off-stage, 38% opacity, blurred to on-stage, 100% opacity, and clear. Scrub through the timeline to see the effect.

5. Ease the Tweening

Right now, the motion is even from start to finish. To change the motion, so that he starts slowly and speeds up or vice versa, change the Easing in the Properties Inspector. Choose a positive Ease value to start out fast and slow down; choose a negative value to start out slow and speed up. To see the difference, test it with 72 and –68. I've chosen –68 for my final Ease value, because that's the effect I like best.

> **T I P**
>
> **Quick Preview.** You can quickly see the effect of your changes by pressing Enter so that Flash moves through the timeline. However, for a more accurate, real-time preview, press Ctrl+Enter (Windows) or Cmd+Enter (Mac OS).

6. Add Final Touches

We've got a pretty nice effect, but we can add some final touches to polish it up a bit. For example, a flash of light just as he arrives at the final position draws provides nice punctuation to the motion. And the little vignette on the Feet layer adds some elegance.

To add the flash of light, add two keyframes just after frame 14. Press F6 twice to add the keyframes. Select the middle keyframe, click on the image, and then change the Color to Brightness in the Properties Inspector. Crank the Brightness up to about 58% **A**. Preview the movie to see the flash of light.

To add the Feet layer, make it visible at layer 14. This is a subtle touch that gives Kaysar a base. ▥

COLIN SMITH

Animated Page Transitions

Use masks and animation to create transitions that shimmer, wipe, or fade in.

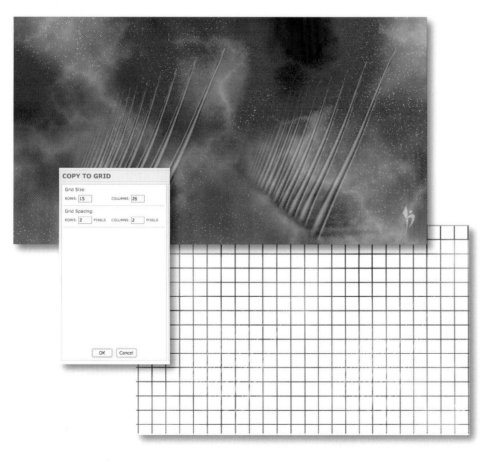

1. Create a Grid

To create a custom transition, we'll start by creating a grid. Open the Transition_start.fla file from the How to Wow CD. There are three layers in the file. Select Layer 3. Holding down the Shift key to constrain it, use the Rectangle tool to draw a small square in the upper-left corner. Make sure there is no stroke; any fill color is fine.

We've drawn a small square; we'll let Flash duplicate it to create an entire grid. Select the square with the Selection tool, and choose Insert > Timeline Effects > Assistants > Copy to Grid.

In the Copy to Grid dialog box, specify a number of rows and columns to fill the entire stage. I need 15 rows and 26 columns, based on the size of the square I drew. Click Update Preview. Flash displays the grid over the stage. You may need to adjust the number of rows and columns a few times to cover the stage. When you're satisfied, click OK. Flash applies the grid.

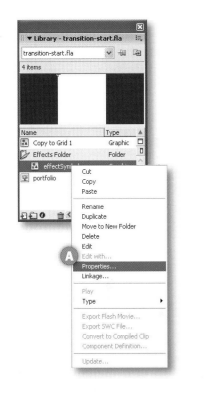

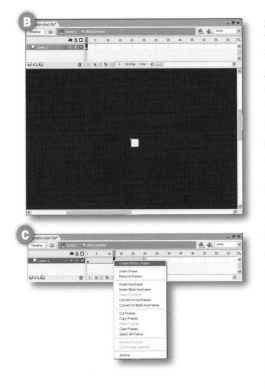

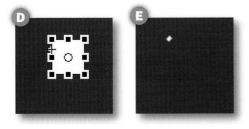

2. Animate the Grid

We want to create an animated transition. Because every square in this grid is an instance of the same master symbol, effectSymbol, we only need to animate one square to affect them all.

First, convert effectSymbol from a graphic symbol into a movie clip symbol. Right-click (Windows) or Control-click (Mac OS) effectSymbol in the Effects folder in the library **A**, and choose Properties. In the Symbol Properties dialog box, select Movie Clip. Convert the Copy to Grid symbol the same way.

Double-click effectSymbol in the library to edit it and open its timeline **B**. Select frame 25 and press F6 to create a keyframe **C**. We want to change the appearance of the symbol over time, so right-click on the timeline between the keyframes and choose Create Motion Tween. Then, select frame 25, and select the Free Transform tool. Enlarge the symbol slightly so that the symbols will overlap **D**. Select the first frame. Zoom into 400%, and then shrink the symbol and rotate it a bit **E**. Scrub the timeline from frame 1 to 25 to see the symbol change from a tiny diamond shape to a larger square.

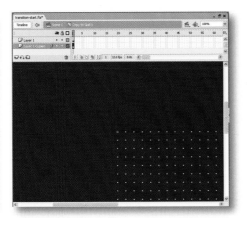

3. Apply the Grid to the Scene

We've animated the grid. Now, let's return to Scene 1 to apply it. First, delete the grid that currently appears on the stage. Then, double-click the Copy to Grid symbol in the library. Flash warns us that we won't be able to edit the settings of the timeline effect. We won't need to edit the settings, so click OK.

The Copy to Grid symbol, a black field with dots, opens.

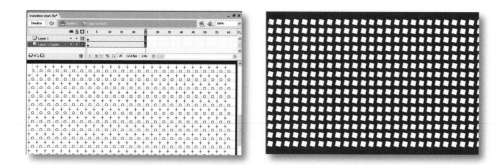

Drag the scroll bars to center the grid so you can see it better. Currently, the symbol has just one frame, but we need to enable 25 frames for the animation. Select frame 25 for both layers, and press F5 to fill them. Now as we scrub through the timeline, we see the full transition effect.

4. Add a Stop Action

Currently, the transition will loop, but we only want to play it once. So we'll need to add a stop action. Select frame 25 and press F6 to add a keyframe. Open the Actions panel. Its header should say Actions-Frame because we're applying an action to a specific frame.

Click Script Assist. Under Global Functions, select Timeline Control, and then double-click Stop to apply it. That's all there is to it. Now, close the Actions panel and return to Scene 1.

5. Apply the Mask

Drag Copy the Grid from the library onto the stage, centering it so that it will cover the entire stage when it expands **A**. Right-click (Windows) or Control-click (Mac OS) the Copy to Grid layer in the Timeline, and choose Mask. Drag the Bg layer into the mask, so that it's nested as well **B**. Now we're ready to test the transition. Press Ctrl+Enter (Windows) or Cmd+Return (Mac OS) to test it. ▥

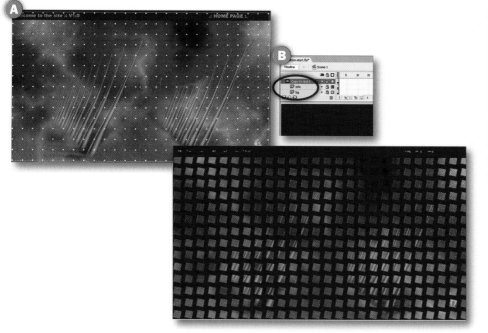

COLIN SMITH

Logo Sheen

Bring metallic surfaces to life using an animated gradient.

1. Create the Gradient

You can use this technique on any object that you want to highlight. The Logo-shine.fla file on the How to Wow CD includes a PNG graphic of a logo I created in Photoshop. This is a metallic logo, but I used blue-gray colors in Photoshop so that I could animate the highlights in Flash to give it a true metallic look.

To create the metallic look, we'll animate a gradient. First zoom out to about 25%, and then create a new layer called Gradient. With the Rectangle tool, draw a long rectangle from one end of the stage to the other. Click the Fill icon and select the black and white gradient.

Move the gradient so that its left edge is near the left edge of the logo, and then, using the Free Transform tool, extend the gradient to the right.

2. Customize the Gradient

Currently, the gradient moves from white to black. To make it appear that light is moving over the logo, we need to create bands of lighter color in the gradient. Select the gradient and open the Color Mixer.

Click the gradient bar in a few places to add color pointers; add a few that are closer to the white side and a few that are closer to the black side. Now, move the pointers to alternate the colors between dark and light.

Let's change the very first pointer to black: select it, and then move the color slider to the bottom. Adjust all the pointers to create dark areas on the edges and multiple sheens that will work for the animation. The black ends will help ensure that the animation loops seamlessly.

Now, change the angle of the gradient so that it looks more realistic. Select the gradient with the Gradient Transform tool, and then drag out the corner handle to create an angle. Let's also pull it to the right a bit, so that its left edge is across the middle of the logo, so that it's dark at the beginning of the animation.

3. Apply a Blending Mode

To use the gradient effectively, we need to apply a blending mode, which will only work with a movie clip symbol. Select the gradient, and press F8. In the Convert to Symbol dialog box, select Movie Clip and name it Sheen. Choose a blending mode from the Blending menu. Zoom in to see the effect more clearly. Overlay provides a highlight without affecting the logo's colors.

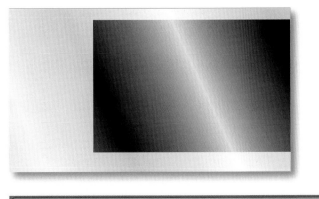

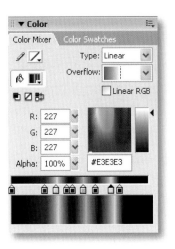

T I P

Expanding Pasteboard. In Flash 8, the Pasteboard automatically expands as you push content outside the current boundaries.

4. Animate the Gradient

The gradient should move across the logo from one end to the other. Select frame 40 and press F6 to add a keyframe. Right-click (Windows) or Control-click (Mac OS) between the keyframes and choose Create Motion Tween.

Select frame 40. Holding down the Shift key, drag the gradient across to the left until the right edge of the gradient is aligned with the right edge of the logo. If you scrub through the timeline now, the gradient moves.

The logo only appears on frame 1, because there are no other frames defined for its layer. To create frames for it, click frame 40 on Layer 1 and press F5. Now as you scrub through the timeline, you can see how the sheen affects the logo.

To test the effect, press Ctrl+Enter (Windows) or Cmd+Return (Mac OS). The animation gives a nice metallic look, but it's moving a little too fast, and there's a flash at the seam.

5. Make Adjustments, As Needed

To edit the gradient, double-click it. Reposition the color pointers in the Color Mixer panel, narrowing the bands of light color to remove the black seam. Return to Scene 1 and test the animation again to ensure that the animation doesn't appear to jump or flash at the seam.

To slow down the animation, add frames. Select a frame in both layers, such as frame 25, and press F5. Each time you press F5, you add a frame. Add 30 or 40 frames to slow the animation significantly. ▥

COLIN SMITH

Shimmering Metal

A moving sparkle of light adds interest to static objects, whether they're cars, electronics, or text.

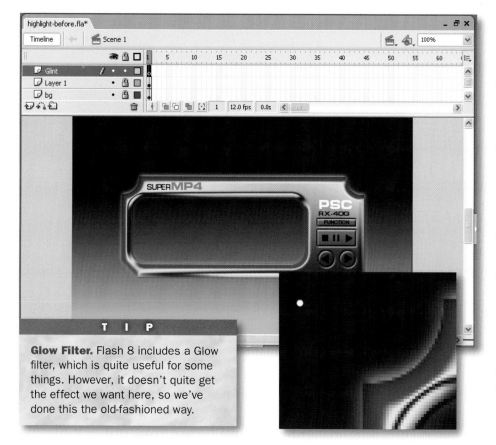

TIP

Glow Filter. Flash 8 includes a Glow filter, which is quite useful for some things. However, it doesn't quite get the effect we want here, so we've done this the old-fashioned way.

1. Create the Glint

That little sparkle that travels around the edge of car, words, or even a tooth is meant to show how clean or snazzy something is. You can give an object that same sparkle in Flash. The Highlight_before.fla file on the How to Wow CD contains an interface that I created in Photoshop. It's a static image, and a glint of light moving around the corner and over the top will make the interface more intriguing.

Create a new layer, called Glint. The glint won't be very large, so zoom in 400% to work with it. Select the Oval tool, with no stroke and a white fill. Holding down the Shift key, draw a very small circle. It should be a small dot. It will look more like a glint of light when we soften the edges. Select the circle with the Selection tool, and then choose Modify > Shape > Soften Fill Edges. In the Soften Fill Edges dialog box, select Expand and set the values for 12 pixels and 12 steps. You can experiment with different values for different glow effects.

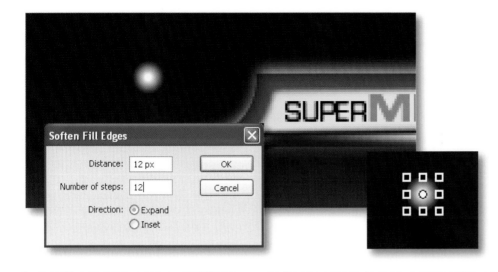

Click away from the circle. There's quite a glow, and now the circle appears to be too big. Use the Free Transform tool to shrink it further.

Scale it down to the size that looks right for the image you're working with.

Now, select the circle and press F8 to convert it to a symbol. Name the symbol Glint, select Movie Clip for the type, and select the center registration point.

2. Add a Motion Guide

We want the glint to move along the curve and across the top of the interface. We'll create a motion guide to lead it. Right-click (Windows) or Control-click (Mac OS) the Glint layer, and then choose Add Motion Guide.

Flash creates a new layer called Guide: Glint, with a motion guide icon on it.

Lock the Glint layer to ensure you don't accidentally edit it, and then hide it so it's not a distraction. Choose the first keyframe for the Guide: Glint layer, because we'll create the motion guide on this layer. Select the Pen tool. Click at the first tip of the curve on the left side and drag it across.

Then click at the end of the curve. Now click at the end of the top edge to add a line all the way across.

I zoomed out to see the edge of the interface. Lock the Guide: Glint layer to ensure you don't move the motion guide.

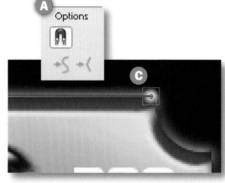

INSIGHT

Straightening the Line. If the top curves rather than being straight, use the Pen tool to fix it. Click once on the Pen tool to change modes. The icon changes to a pen nib with a v. Click on the corner to convert it to a sharp corner, automatically straightening the line across the top.

3. Animate the Sparkle

Now that the motion guide is in place, display and unlock the Glint layer. Select the glint and drag it to the beginning of the motion guide. Make sure the Snap to Objects button is enabled in the Tools panel **A**. Next, we'll add some frames for the animation. Select frame 12 for all the layers in the timeline, and then press F5 to create the frames **B**. Then, select frame 12 for just the Glint layer and press F6 to create a keyframe. Right-click (Windows) or Control-click (Mac OS) between the keyframes and choose Create Motion Tween.

Move the playhead to frame 12, and then drag the glint to the end of the top edge of the interface, its final position. It should snap to the end of the motion guide **C**. Deselect the glint. Scrub through the timeline to see the glint move along the motion guide. To test the animation, press Ctrl+Enter (Windows) or Cmd+Return (Mac OS).

4. Tweak the Animation

Now, the glint moves along the motion guide, but its pace is too steady. There's no acceleration or deceleration. Additionally, it's looping too frequently.

First, let's make the motion more realistic. Move the playhead to the point that the glint almost gets to the top, and then press F6 to add a keyframe.

We've split the animation into two parts. The first part controls the curve and the second controls the straight line. Select the first frame and press F5 twice to add frames, slowing the animation over the curve. To make the glint decelerate as it goes across the top, click the new keyframe and then, in the Properties Inspector, set the Easing to 60.

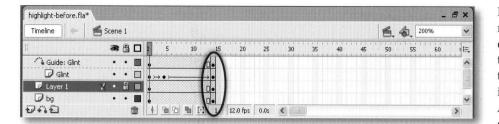

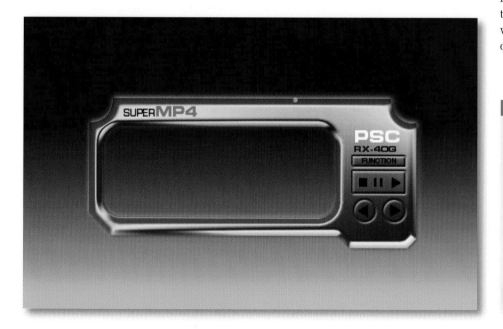

If you scrub through the timeline, you'll notice that only the glint shows at the end because we added frames to only the Glint layer. To add frames to each of the other layers, click on the last frame in the layer and drag it to the right. All the layers have the same number of frames.

To deal with the frequent looping, we'll add more frames, but only to the bg and Layer 1 layers. Shift-click to select both layers, and then press F5 repeatedly to add about 50 frames. These frames will add a "pause" to the motion by providing a period of time where no motion is taking place. Test the glint's animation again, and keep adjusting until the timing is right.

Preview and enjoy the final result. This type of effect is also used frequently on web pages to add some movement to an otherwise static background image.

Freehand Writing

As if guided by an invisible hand, writing appears across the screen.

1. Write the Text

In a Flash document, write the text as you want it to appear at the end of the animation. Use the Paintbrush or Pencil tool for best results, selecting the appropriate brush size and stroke shape. Writing with a mouse can be awkward; you'll have better results if you use a graphics tablet. I'm using the Signature_ start.fla file off the How to Wow CD.

2. Work Backwards, Erasing Gradually

Create a keyframe for the final image. For a simple word, 40 frames is about right. Select the frame and press F6 to create the keyframe. Now, select frame 40 and, pressing the Alt (Windows) or Option (Mac OS) key, drag the keyframe back to frame 38. Then, use the Eraser tool to erase the last stroke written. In the sample signature, the last stroke would have been crossing the "t."

Next, select the keyframe and press Alt or Option to drag it back a frame or two. Continue erasing a stroke or two each time you create a keyframe. Pressing Alt or Option as you drag the keyframe copies the contents of the current keyframe so you don't have to erase sections all over again. When you get to the first keyframe, delete the entire text object.

TIP

Vary the Writing Speed. Some letters take longer to craft than others. A long, smooth stroke goes quickly, but a lowercase "a" can take some time. How quickly the writing appears on screen depends on how much you erase per frame, and how many frames you skip. The more frames you move at a time, the slower the writing.

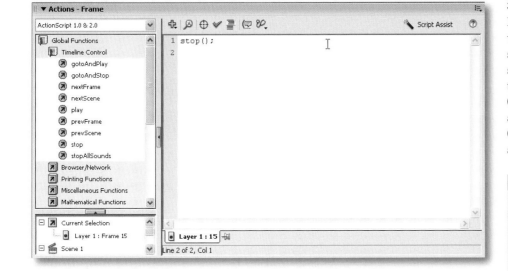

3. Add a Stop Action

By default, Flash loops movies, but we want the writing to appear and then stop on the screen. So we need to add a stop action. Select the final frame. Open the Actions panel. Choose Timeline Controls, and then double-click Stop to apply it. Press Ctrl+Enter (Windows) or Cmd+Return (Mac OS) to test the animation.

TIP

Time saver. Rather than dragging each keyframe, create the entire animation backwards so that the signature slowly dissapears. Select the entire animation in the timeline, right click your mouse and choose > Reverse Frames.

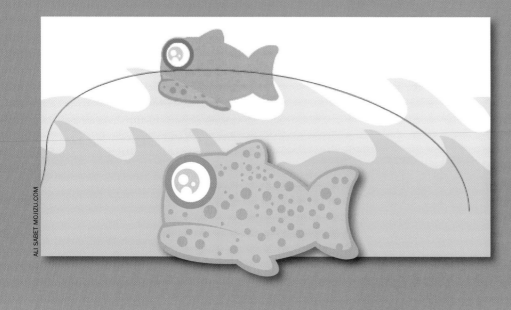

ALI SABET MOJIZU.COM

Motion on a Path

Take your animations off the beaten path. Move them along a motion guide, transforming them to face the appropriate direction as they go.

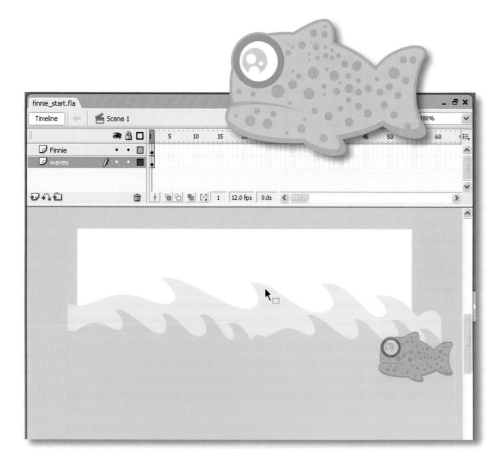

1. Animate the Object

Meet Finnie, a fish with an attitude drawn by my friend Ali Sabet (founder of www.mojizu.com). We'll make Finnie leap into the air, return to the water, and swim away. Open Finnie_start.fla from the How to Wow CD. Lock the Waves layer, because we won't be making any changes to it.

Now, create the basic animation. We'll move Finnie across the screen in about 25 frames, so select frame 25 for both layers and press F5 to create the frames. Then, select frame 25 for the Finnie layer, and press F6 to create a keyframe. Right-click (Windows) or Control-click (Mac OS) between the keyframes and choose Create Motion Tween. Select frame 25 and move Finnie to the left side of the stage. Now, when you scrub through the timeline, Finnie moves from the right side of the stage to the left.

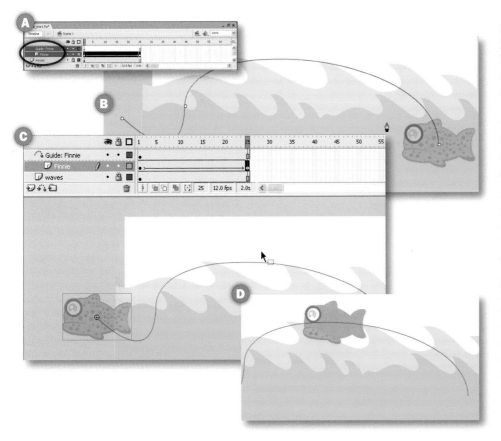

2. Add a Motion Guide

Finnie's getting where he needs to go, but he can do it with more style. We'll create a motion guide for him to follow as he leaps out of the water. Right-click (Windows) or Control-click (Mac OS) on the Finnie layer, and choose Add Motion Guide. Flash adds the Guide: Finnie layer and nests the Finnie layer beneath it **A**.

To create the guide, select the first frame, and then, with the Pen tool, draw the guide. I've created an initial arc and then a little extra at the end so that he can swim away **B**.

We need to snap Finnie to the motion guide at each end for him to follow it. Make sure the Snap to Objects button is enabled. Then, with frame 1 selected, snap Finnie to the right end of the motion guide. And with frame 25 selected, snap Finnie to the left end of the motion guide **C**.

Scrub through the timeline to ensure that Finnie is following the path **D**.

3. Transform the Object

Currently, Finnie is facing the same direction the entire way. Of course, when a fish jumps, its head goes first. So, select the first frame, and then select Finnie with the Free Transform tool. Rotate Finnie so he's facing the path.

Now Finnie starts out facing up, and gradually moves to a horizontal position, so he hits the water with his belly. Let's make another adjustment to smooth that out. Select the last frame and rotate Finnie so he's facing down.

Depending on your level of perfectionism, you may want to continue to tweak Finnie's position at different points in the animation, but I think Finnie looks pretty good.

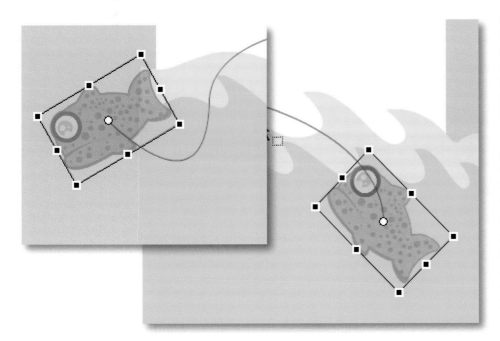

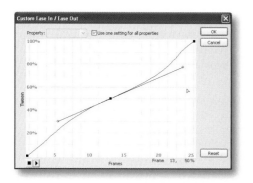

4. Add a Stop Action

Finnie could be stuck swimming the same path over and over again, jumping back to the beginning each time. We'll stop him after his first swim, though. Create a new layer called Actions and drag it above all the other layers.

Select frame 25 in the Actions layer and press F6 to create a keyframe. Then open the Actions panel. Select Global Functions > Timeline Control, and then double-click Stop to apply it. Now the animation will play once and stop.

5. Adjust the Easing

In the real world, a fish wouldn't jump out of the water and dive back in at a consistent speed. We can use the custom easing feature in Flash to alter Finnie's speed accordingly. Select Finnie, and select the first frame. In the Properties Inspector, click Edit next to the Ease field.

The Custom Ease In/Ease Out dialog box contains the easing curve. It begins as a straight diagonal line, with the motion at a consistent speed.

To change the speed, we'll change the shape of the curve. Click the Play button in the bottom corner of the dialog box to play the animation and identify where you want the speed to change. It's just about frame 13 where we want Finnie to be at his slowest point, just as he reaches the top of his leap. In the Custom Ease In/Ease Out dialog box, click on the curve at frame 13 to create a handle. Drag that handle to adjust the curve, and then play the animation to see the effect. You can adjust it as many times as necessary.

INSIGHT

Color Changes. When Finnie comes out of the water, he changes color. That's because I've applied a Multiply blending mode to the object. Blending modes affect how layers interact with each other. The Multiply blending mode multiplies the colors together, making them darker, when the layer is darker than 50% gray, and it has no effect when the layer is lighter than 50% gray. So, under the water, Finnie is darker, and above the water, he's pure orange.

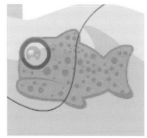

Unrolling a Scroll

Reveal an image with a flourish: create the illusion of unrolling a scroll of paper.

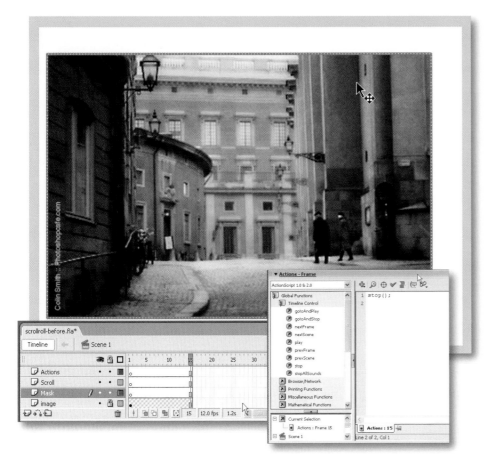

1. Set Up the File

This transition effect works well when you want to reveal a photograph or other image. We'll use an image I shot in Stockholm, Sweden; it's already in the Scrollroll_before.fla file on the How to Wow CD. Open the file, and then drag the photo from the library onto the stage.

Let's add 15 frames. Select frame 15, and then press F5 to fill in the frames. Lock the Image layer so that you won't disturb the image as you work. Then, create three new layers: Actions, Scroll, and Mask.

We know that we want to run the animation once and then stop with the image fully displayed. So, let's create a stop action. Select the last frame in the Actions layer, and press F6 to create a keyframe. Then open the Actions panel. Select Global Functions and Timeline Control. Double-click Stop. Flash adds the stop action. That's the only action we'll add for this project, so you can close the Actions panel.

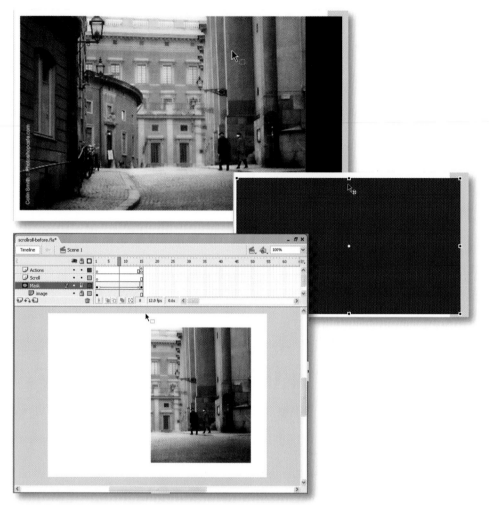

2. Create the Mask

The key to this effect is using an animated mask that gradually reveals more of the image. We'll create that mask now. Select the first frame in the Mask layer. Then select the Rectangle tool, with no stroke and a black fill. Now, draw a narrow, tall rectangle next to the image. Select frame 15 in the Mask layer, and press F6 to create a keyframe. Using the Free Transform tool, drag the rectangle across so that it covers the image. To create the shape tween, select the first frame, open the Properties Inspector, and choose Shape from the Tween menu.

Now, as you scrub through the timeline, the black rectangle expands to cover the image. Of course, we actually want the opposite to happen—we want to see more of the image as time passes. The black rectangle will serve as a mask, so that only the area it covers is visible. Right-click (Windows) or Control-click (Mac OS) the Mask layer and choose Mask.

Flash locks the Mask layer and nests the Image layer under it to indicate that it's masked. As you scrub through the timeline, more of the image appears.

3. Create the Scroll

We have the image, but we're missing the scroll. We'll create that next. Unlock the Mask layer to see the image, and then select the first frame in the Scroll layer. Draw a rectangle on top of the first rectangle, but a little wider.

We'll add a gradient to make the rectangle look like it's rolled paper. Open the Color Mixer panel. Click the Fill Color icon, and select the black and white linear gradient. The default gradient has two color pointers, white on one end

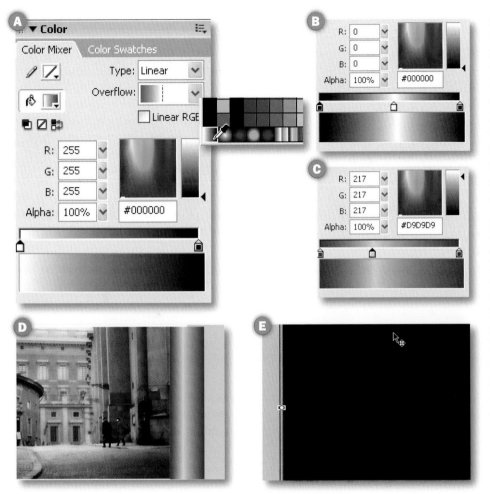

and black on the other **A**. Press the Alt (Windows) or Option (Mac OS) key and drag a copy of the black pointer all the way to the left, and then drag the white color pointer to the middle **B**. Each end of the gradient is black and the middle is white. Lighten the black and darken the white a little bit, to create less contrast. The goal is to make this look like rolled paper **C**, **D**.

The roll of paper needs to move across the stage as we unroll the image—and, as the paper unrolls, the scroll should become smaller. Select the final frame and press F6 to create a keyframe. Drag the rectangle to the other side of the image **E**. Right-click (Windows) or Control-click (Mac OS) between the keyframes in the timeline and choose Create Motion Tween. Then, use the Free Transform tool to resize it so that it's very narrow.

Lock the Mask layer again, and then scrub through the timeline to see the image revealed as the scroll grows smaller.

4. Remove the Scroll from the Last Frame

When a paper is completely unrolled, no scroll should remain. That narrow scroll shouldn't appear in the last frame. Unlock the Mask and Scroll layers. Hold down the Shift key as you select the last frame in each layer. Then drag the keyframes back to frame 14. Now, select frame 15 for the Mask and Scroll layers, and press Shift+F5 to remove those frames, so that only the Image layer appears in the last frame.

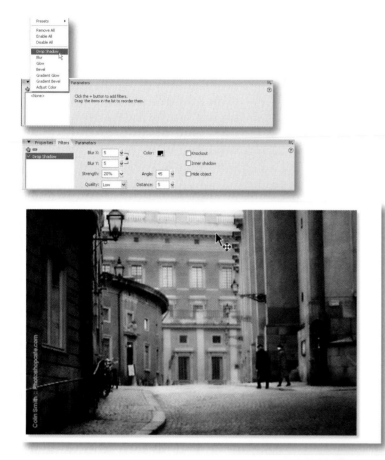

5. Add Drop Shadows for Depth

To make this image seem more three-dimensional, we'll add a drop shadow to it, and one to the scroll as well. The Drop Shadow effect in Flash works with movie clip symbols, so we'll need to convert the image. Unlock the Image layer, and select the photograph. Press F8. In the Convert to Symbol dialog box, select Movie Clip and name the symbol Photo. Open the Filters panel. Click the plus icon, and choose Drop Shadow. Flash creates a drop shadow with the default settings, which you can adjust. Let's drop the Strength down to 20% to create just a slight shadow.

Add a drop shadow to the scroll the same way. Select the Scroll layer and press F8. In the Convert to Symbol dialog box, select Movie Clip and name the symbol Scroll. Double-click the scroll to edit it; select frame 14 and press F5 to fill the frames. Then, open the Filters panel, click the Plus icon, and choose Drop Shadow. Adjust the drop shadow's settings. I've set this to 20% strength to match the other drop shadow. ▨

Masking

In the graphic arts, masking is used to show only a specific area in an image. Masks are especially powerful tools in Flash, because you can animate a mask to reveal an image gradually.

Creating a Mask

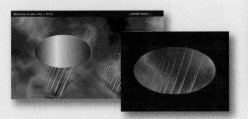

Masking may seem nonintuitive at first. When you create a mask, you initially cover the area that you eventually want to reveal. For example, if you mask an image with a circle, only the area of the image that is under the circle will show in the final movie. The mask shapes acts as a window. Any filled area is completely transparent in the mask; any area that isn't filled is opaque.

Create a new layer, and then draw your masking shape. You can use any of the drawing tools in Flash to create a mask shape, as well as a type object, an instance of a graphic symbol, or even a movie clip. However, a mask layer can only contain one masking object.

Position the mask layer directly above the layer that contains the object you want to partially hide or slowly reveal. Then, right-click (Windows) or Control-click (Mac OS) the mask layer, and choose Mask. Flash automatically links the mask layer to the layer beneath it, nesting the lower layer. It also automatically locks the mask layer, revealing the object below. You can unlock the mask layer and reposition the mask over a different area of the masked object; while the layer is unlocked, you cannot see the effect of the mask.

Animating a Mask

Because a mask controls how much of an image is revealed, animating a mask lets you reveal parts of an image over time. For example, in the scroll project, we use a mask to reveal the image as it appears to be unrolling. In the animated page transitions, we enlarge the mask shape over time to increase the amount of the image that is revealed, until the entire image is shown.

To animate a mask, first create the initial mask layer, covering the part of the image that you want to appear at the beginning of the animation. Then create a keyframe for the end of the animation, and transform the mask to show the part of the image you want to reveal then. Then, as with most animations, create a tween to change the mask over time. 🖮

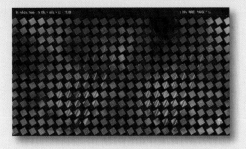

4

SPECIAL EFFECTS

Everyone loves those cool little effects that make something go from average to wow!

OPTIMIZING RASTER GRAPHICS *86*

AUTOMATING REPETITIVE TASKS *87*

FROM PHOTO TO HAND-PAINTED AND BACK *88*

ANIMATED OUTLINE TO OBJECT *91*

SMOKE AND STEAM *96*

REFLECTIONS *100*

IMPORTING 3D ANIMATION *103*

SPECIAL EFFECTS ARE NOTHING new. People have been using physical props to achieve moods and create illusions for a very long time, from moving a jar of colored liquid in front of a candle to suspending bats from strings in the early Dracula movies. But digital capabilities have taken special effects to previously unimagined levels, so that almost any illusion is possible now.

The audience oohs and aahs at the movie theater when special effects are done particularly well, so that viewers can suspend their disbelief and travel to surreal places or witness events that would be difficult, if not impossible, to capture with the camera. Of course, special effects aren't just for movie theaters. Have you visited a website and seen some small thing that made you say "wow"?

Special effects can't make up for poor design, but they can make the difference between a satisfactory experience and one that is sublime. You can make even your most jaded viewers smile by providing an unexpected treat.

This chapter discloses the secrets to some standard and some not-so-standard special effects, some including motion and some that don't need to move to knock your socks off. We'll transform a photograph to look like hand-painted illustration, and then, like magic, fade it into the photograph. We'll send a dash around the shape of an object and then, poof!, the object will appear in a blur of glory.

You'll learn to create a sense of atmosphere, taking advantage of blending modes and animation to produce smoke or steam effects that look so realistic you'll reach for the fire extinguisher. Subtle motion like this can make a static photograph look like a video. A small amount of motion goes a long way.

Reflected logos and images are all over the web lately. It's a cool effect, and as you'll soon learn, it's also an easy one.

Visual effects expert Michael Donnellan was generous enough to share his tips with us, as well. He'll show you how to import 3D objects into Flash to create amazing websites like the ones he produces for the entertainment industry.

As always, I encourage you to take in the essence of these projects and then personalize them. Experiment with the principles, change various settings, and see what kind of effects you can come up with yourself. I think you'll enjoy working through this chapter as much as I enjoyed creating it. I know you'll enjoy getting your hands dirty with these projects. All the source files are included on the CD.

Optimizing Raster Graphics

If you work with imported raster, or bitmap, graphics in Flash, you'll want to optimize them to achieve the smallest file size without compromising quality. Once you've got a feel for optimization, you can apply the settings quickly using the History Panel in Flash.

About Image Compression

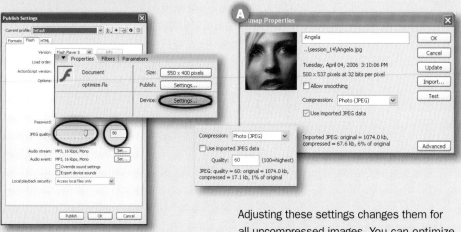

Bitmap images, which are pixel based, can become very large in file size. And when you're creating files for a web audience, you want to keep your file size as small as possible, enabling short download times. Compression, which dramatically reduces an image's file size, is essential.

Flash handles bitmap images pretty well. If you import a compressed images such as JPEG, or GIF image, Flash makes no initial attempt to re-compress it because twice compressed images don't look too good as a rule. However, by default, Flash tries to compress uncompressed images such as PNG and Tif images. To see how Flash is compressing images globaly, open the Properties inspector and click Settings next to Publish. In the Publish Settings dialog box, you'll see all the settings Flash is applying to bitmap images when you publish your movies. It converts images to JPEG files and applies the compression.

Adjusting these settings changes them for all uncompressed images. You can optimize images individually, rather than relying on Flash to blanket the same settings across the board. For example, if you're using an image sequence you may want to use a higher compression than you would on a single still image, because they are displayed for such as short time.

To set compression values for an individual bitmap graphic, double-click it in the Library panel or click the properties icon. The Bitmap Properties dialog box opens. You can drag the preview image to see a different section of it; in this image, all I saw was background until I dragged Angela's face into view **A**.

By default, Flash uses the imported JPEG data. Deselect that option and change the Quality setting. Click Test to see what it looks like in the preview window. If you lower the Quality setting, you'll reduce the file size, but the photo may suffer. You will need to balance quality with file size. Beneath the Quality setting, Flash displays the new file size. Click OK when you're ready to apply the settings. ▦

Automating Repetitive Tasks

When you have hundreds of images that you would like to optimize, you begin to wonder if threre's an easier way to do this. Luckily for you, your reading the solutuion right now.

Optimizing Raster Graphics

Optimizing each image individually can be tedious. To apply the settings quickly, use the History panel. The History panel records every action you take in Flash, and you can replay actions in any order.

To open the History panel, choose Windows > Other Panels > History. Flash recorded the image optimization as Bitmap Properties, and it recorded the exact settings we used. To apply the same settings to another image, select that image and press Replay in the History panel.

If you expect to use those settings frequently, create a command. Select Bitmap Properties in the History panel, and click the Save icon at the bottom of the History panel **A**. Name the command something you'll understand later, such as "Optimize to 60," and click OK. Your custom command appears in the Commands menu.

Custom Shortcuts

You can make your life even easier by creating custom keyboard shortcuts for the commands you create—or for any other commands you use frequently. Choose Edit > Keyboard Shortcuts. Flash includes several default keyboard shortcut sets. To customize your own, you'll need to duplicate one of them. Click the Duplicate Set icon, and name the new set. Then, navigate to the command for which you want to add or change a shortcut, and press the actual shortcut keys below. Flash will warn you if the shortcut is already assigned to another command. Click Change to apply the new shortcut. ⌨

COLIN SMITH

From Photo to Hand-Painted and Back

A hand-painted image fades into a full photograph.

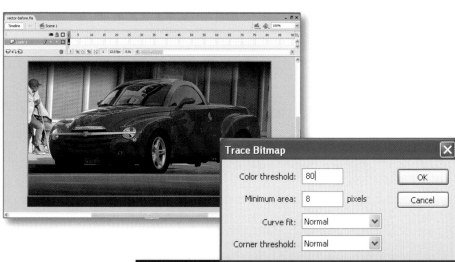

1. Trace the Bitmap

Start with a copy of the photograph. I've opened the Vector_before.fla file from the How to Wow CD. The file contains a photograph of a car, but you can use this effect with any photograph. To create the hand-painted version of the image, we'll use the Trace Bitmap feature. Select the image, and choose Modify > Bitmap > Trace Bitmap. In the Trace Bitmap dialog box, set the Color Threshold to 80, Minimum Area to 8, and both Curve Fit and Corner Threshold to Normal.

When you click OK, Flash traces the bitmap, creating a vector version of the image. This is a processor-intensive effect, so you may have to wait a minute for Flash to make its computations. Click elsewhere on the screen to deselect the image.

After Flash finishes tracing the bitmap, the scene looks as if it has been painted by hand. Click the keyframe to select the image, and press F8. In the Convert to Symbol, name it Vector and select Movie Clip.

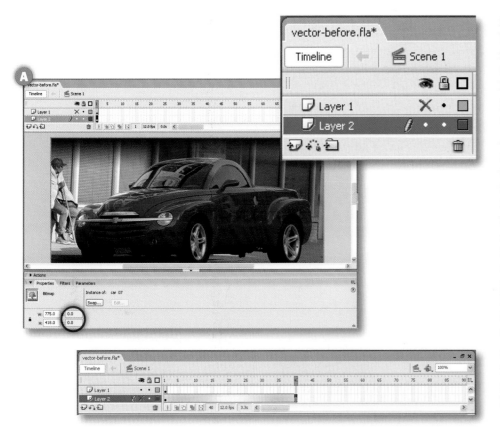

2. Add the Photograph

We'll fade the vector version of the image into the original photograph. Create a new layer, and drag it beneath Layer 1. Hide Layer 1. Drag the photograph from the Library panel onto the stage.

Align the photograph with the symbol exactly, so that when the symbol fades, the same part of the photograph shows through. The easiest way to align the images is to use the Properties Inspector. Select the photo you just dragged onto the stage. Then, in the Properties inspector, type 0 for the x and y coordinates **A**. The upper-left corner of the photograph will align with the upper-left corner of the stage. Now hide Layer 2 and show Layer 1. Select layer 1, and set its x and y coordinates, too.

Currently, both images are on only one frame. Select frame 40 for Layer 2 and press F5 to create frames. The effect will be 40 frames long, with a slow fade.

3. Fade the Hand-Painted Layer

We'll animate the symbol layer so that it becomes more transparent, revealing the photograph beneath it. Select frame 25 of Layer 1 and press F6 to create a keyframe. Show both layers. Right-click (Windows) or Control-click (Mac OS) between the keyframes on Layer 1, and choose Create Motion Tween. Select the new keyframe, and then click on the image. In the Properties Inspector, change the Color to Alpha, and then set it to 0%, making the image completely transparent.

Trace Bitmap Settings. When Flash traces a bitmap, it's actually converting the image into a vector graphic with separate, editable areas of color.

Color Threshold: You can enter any value between 1 and 500; higher thresholds decrease the number of colors and make the resulting image look less like a photograph.

Minimum Area: This setting determines how many of the surrounding pixels Flash considers when it assigns a color to a pixel. You can enter any value between 1 and 1000, but larger values will cause Flash to process extremely slowly, and in my experience, lower values work just fine.

Curve Fit: This setting determines how smoothly Flash draws the outlines of the converted image.

Corner Threshold: This setting determines whether sharp edges are retained or smoothed out.

At this point, the sketch will slowly morph into the real photograph from frames 1 to 25. But the painted version is too cool to have it fade right away. Let's have it stay on the screen for 15 frames before it begins to fade. Shift-click to select all the frames in Layer 1, and then drag the selected layer to the right in the timeline, move them between frames 15 and 40. Now the image will begin to fade at frame 15, but there's nothing between frames 1 and 15. Select frame 15, press Alt, and drag frame 15 to frame 1 to duplicate frame 15 in frames 1–14.

Now the sketch will appear, remain for 15 frames, and then slowly fade, revealing the photograph.

4. Add a Stop Action

We only want this animation to play once, so we need to add our old friend, the stop action to the last frame. First, create a new layer named Actions. Then, select the last frame in that layer and press F6 to create a keyframe. In the Actions panel, select Global Functions and then Timeline Control. Then, double-click Stop to add the stop action. Close the Action panel.

We're ready to test the animation. Press Ctrl+Enter (Windows) or Cmd+Return (Mac OS) to see how it looks. 🎞

Animated Outline to Object

To build suspense, trace the outline of an object before it appears.

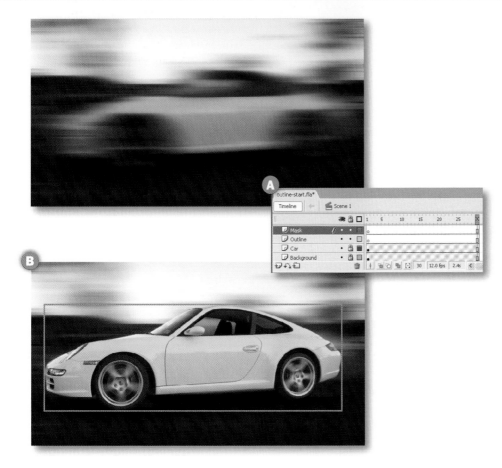

1. Create Layers

Eventually, we'll show an object on the background. Before it appears, though, we'll run an outline around the object, and then flash the entire outline. I've opened Outline-start.fla, which is included on the How to Wow CD. For this project, we'll use the car in the library.

Rename Layer 1 "Background." Then, select frame 30 and press F5 to add 30 frames to the timeline **A**. Now, lock the layer. We won't need to make any changes to it.

Create another layer called "Car." Drag the car from the library onto the background and position it to line up with the blurred car in the background **B**. While the car is selected, press F8. In the Convert to Symbol dialog box, name the symbol Car and select Movie Clip for the type. Lock the Car layer.

Create another layer called "Outline," and a fourth layer called "Mask."

2. Draw the Outline

Next we'll actually need to draw the outline around the car. Select the Outline layer. Then, select the Pen tool, with a white stroke and no fill.

It's probably easiest to start at the top of the windshield. Click the Pen tool at the top, and then click again at the bottom of the windshield, dragging a little to create a curve. It doesn't have to be perfect.

Continue clicking around the car, including the wheels, to create the full outline of the car. If you're not experienced with the Pen tool, you may need to practice a bit to get a sense of how the curve changes when you drag the end. The more you use it, the better you get. To remove the last segment you drew, press Ctrl+Z (Windows) or Cmd+Z (Mac OS). When you reach your starting point, double-click to close the outline.

Now, clean up any irregular areas in the outline. Select the Selection tool. As you move it near the line, the icon changes. When an arc displays, you can change the curve of the line. Click and drag the outline segments to smooth them out. It doesn't have to be absolutely perfect, because the outline will only appear on screen briefly, but it should approximate the outline of the car. Hide the Car layer to see the outline clearly.

3. Mask the Outline

Double-click the entire outline, and in the Properties inspector, make sure the stroke is a solid 3-pixels **A**.

To create the illusion that the outline is moving around the car, we'll mask a small area. Now, select the Mask layer. We'll use a simple rectangle for the mask. Select the Rectangle tool, with no

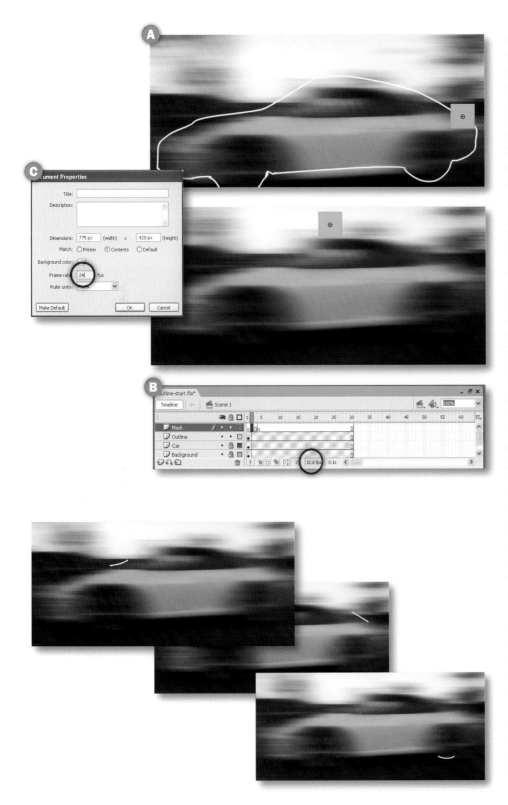

stroke and a bright green fill **A**. Color doesn't really matter as it will be a mask. For now choose something that's easy to see. Draw a rectangle. The size of the rectangle determines how much of the line will show at a time. We'll start the outline at the back of the car. Press F8 to convert the rectangle to a movie clip symbol; it's fine to leave it named Symbol 1.

The mask is already in position at the back of the car. Select frame 4 and press F6 to create a keyframe. Then, move the mask to the top of the car. Right-click between the two keyframes and choose Create Motion Tween. Scrub through frames 1 to 4 to see the mask move. It's pretty jerky because we don't have enough avaliable frames for the subtle movements. To smooth it out, we need to provide more frames, so we will increase the frame rate. Double-click the current frame rate **B**, to launch the Document Properties and then type 24 for the new frame rate **C**. So that the movement is smoother but occurs over the same time period, drag the original keyframe from frame 4 to frame 8. And then we need to drag the final keyframes for the Outline, Car, and Background layers out to frame 60.

Gradually move the mask around the car, creating keyframes and motion tweens for each section of the car. You can't mask a motion guide, so the mask will tween in a straight line. Therefore, we need a new keyframe every time the mask should change direction. Continue until you reach the point you started from.

To create the mask itself, right-click (Windows) or Control-click (Mac OS) the Mask layer and choose Mask. Now when you scrub through the timeline, you'll see the outline move around the car.

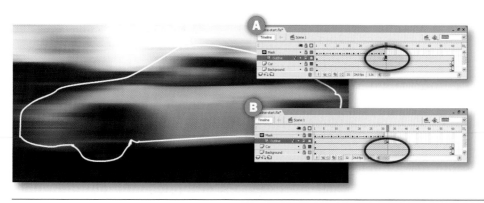

4. Reveal the Full Outline

The last mask frame is frame 30. Next, we want to reveal the full outline for a frame or two. So, select the last keyframe in the Outline layer and move it to frame 31 in that layer **A**. We only want the outline to show for a frame or two, so select frames 33 to 60 of the Outline layer, and then hold down the Shfit key and press F5 to delete the frames **B**.

5. Show the Full Object

Initially, the outline moves around the car. Then, we see the full outline for a couple of frames. Next, we want to show the car. Drag the first keyframe from the Car layer to frame 31, directly beneath the keyframe in the Outline layer **A**.

Let's first show the car with a white fill, and gradually show the photo. Unlock the Car layer, select the car, and open the Properties inspector. Choose Tint from the Color menu, select a fill of white, and set the tint to 100%. The car is filled with white **B**.

Don't worry that it doesn't fit the outline exactly, because this is just going to flash quickly on the screen.

Select frame 35 and press F6 to create another keyframe. Right-click (Windows) or Control-click (Mac OS) between frames 31 and 35, and choose Create Motion Tween. Select frame 35, and change the tint to 10% **C**. Gradually, we'll remove the tint altogether. Add a keyframe to frame 44, and then create a motion tween between frames 35 and 44. Choose None from the Color menu in the Properties inspector. This will fade the white tint over time.

Scrubbing through, we see the outline move around the car, the outline appeara in full with a white fill, and then the outline disappears and the fill fades until we see the car.

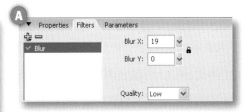

6. Add Finishing Touches

In addition to the white tint, let's add a little blur to change the way the car arrives on the scene. Click frame 31 on the Car layer, open the Filters panel, and select the car. Click the plus sign in the Filters panel and choose Blur. Click the padlock icon to unlock the constrain option on the blur filter. This will enable use to set the x and y blurs individually. Set x to 19 and y to 0 **A**. Select the next keyframe, at frame 35, and make sure the blur is also at 19. Because we already have a motion tween between frames 35 and 44, and because there is no blur in frame 44, the blur will fade out over those frames.

Finally, let's add a stop action so that the animation sequence only occurs once. Add another layer named Actions at the top of the timeline. Create a keyframe on layer 60. Open the Actions panel. Select Global Functions, and then Timeline Control. Double-click Stop to add a stop action. ▥

COLIN SMITH

Smoke and Steam

Add ambience to a scene with smoke or steam. It's not hard to do with nested symbols of a single cloud image.

1. Create the Cloud Image

I shot this interesting photograph of train tracks heading out to sea in San Francisco and retouched it in Photoshop to give it an old-time look. To add atmosphere, we'll create smoke and steam rising up from the ground. I created a cloud image in Photoshop, using the Clouds filter, darkened the edges, and then imported the image into Flash for you. Open the cloud.fla file from the How to Wow CD.

The image is on the bottom layer. Create a new layer called Steam. Drag the Cloud image from the Library onto the stage. Press F8 to convert it to a movie clip symbol called Cloud 1.

2. Add the First Bit of Steam

The initial cloud image is quite large. Resize it with the Free Transform tool to a more realistic size for a puff of steam **A**. Steam doesn't rise with a black background, so we'll apply a blending mode to make that disappear. Open the Properties inspector, and choose Lighten from the Blend menu **B**. The steam already looks much wispier, because only the white remains. (Don't you love the new blend modes in Flash 8!) Move it to the bottom of the image.

3. Animate a Nested Symbol

Double-click the cloud symbol to edit it. We're working with the Cloud 1 symbol's timeline now **A**. We want to animate the cloud inside the symbol. So select the cloud again and press F8 to convert it to a movie clip called Internal 1. Once again, change the blending mode to Lighten **B**.

Now we can animate this internal 1 symbol to move up from the bottom of the photo, with the steam fading away as it rises. Select frame 50 and press F6 to create a keyframe. Then right-click (Windows) or Control-click (Mac OS) between the keyframes and choose Create Motion Tween **C**. Select frame 50 and move the steam all the way to the top of the image. Then we need to make the final steam more transparent. With frame 50 selected, select the steam, and open the Properties inspector. Choose Alpha from the Color menu, and select 0% **D**. Then, select frame 1, move the steam to the very bottom of the image, and change the Alpha value to 44%.

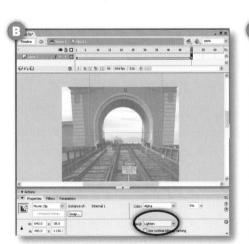

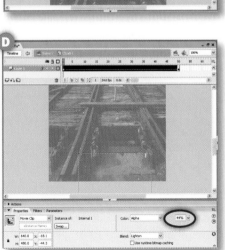

Return to Scene 1. Drag the steam down so that it starts at the very bottom of the image. Press Ctrl+Enter (Windows) or Command+Return (Mac OS) to see how the steam travels. In real life, steam's path widens as it dissipates. Double-click the steam symbol to edit it again. Select frame 50, and then use the Free Transform tool to widen the smoke image. This is a subtle difference but it makes it much more realistic.

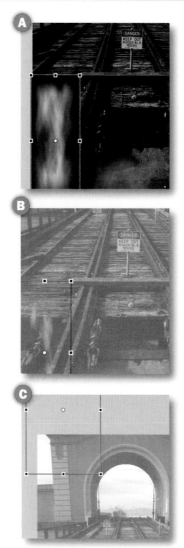

4. Create A Second Puff of Steam

We've got one steam symbol, but we need more. Return to Scene 1. Create another layer named Steam 2. Drag the original Cloud image onto the stage **A**. Resize it to be taller and narrower than the other, and drop it down to the lower-left corner. Then press F8 to convert it to a symbol called Cloud 2. In the Properties Inspector, choose Lighten from the Blend menu. Then, double-click the symbol to edit it, and press F8 to convert it to another movie clip called Internal 2. Once again, apply the Lighten blending mode **B**.

Animate this one the way you did the other, but a little faster, this one will be more of jet of steam. Create a keyframe on frame 40, and create a motion tween between the keyframes. For the first frame, choose an Alpha of 50%. For the final frame, choose an Alpha value of 0%, move the steam to the top of the screen, and widen it a little **C**.

Return to Scene 1. Position the second symbol below the image, a little in from the edge. Now test the project so far. The thinner steam is faster. We're slowly building up our steam and smoke, and by using the same image over and over again as different symbols, we're not adding to the file size.

5. Add More Steam

You've got the idea now. For a more realistic effect, you'd probably want to create 5-10 layers, with opacity low. Create another layer, drag the image onto the stage again, rotate it and resize it, create another movie clip symbol called Steam 3, and set the blending mode to Lighten. Double-click to edit it, create another internal symbol, and set the blending mode to Lighten. For the third one, try using 85 frames, with an original alpha value of 40%. Think about real steam, the slower it moves, the more time is has to dissipate, so fade out the slower moving ones more, faster moving jets of steam won't widen and fade as much as the slower larger bodies of gas. Experiment with each of the additional layers. Be creative! ▥

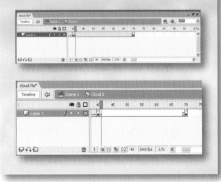

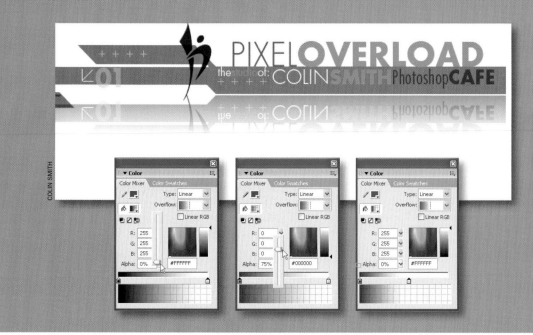

Reflections

Use a transparency gradient mask to realistically reflect any bitmap image, so that it fades as it would in a real reflection.

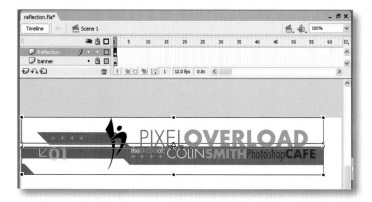

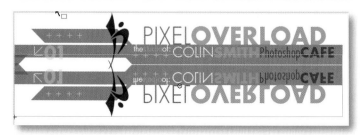

1. Create the Reflection

You can use this effect on any bitmap image. I've opened Reflection.fla, which is on the How to Wow CD. First, we need to convert the bitmap image into a movie clip symbol: select it and press F8. Name the symbol Banner.

We'll leave this original alone and reflect a copy of it. So, choose Copy > Edit to copy the image. Lock the first layer to protect it, and create a new layer called Reflection. Choose Edit > Paste in Place to paste the image in exactly the same place it was on the original layer.

Now, we need to reflect the image. Select it with the Free Transform tool, and then drag the top border down until it switches places with the bottom border.

Keep dragging until the new borders match the original image borders. Now, use the Selection tool to move the reflection below the original image, wherever you want the reflection to appear. The reflection is in place, so lock the layer to keep from accidentally shifting it.

2. Create the Gradient Mask

In the real world, reflections fade. So we need to create a transparency gradient mask. Create a new layer called Mask. Then, use the Rectangle tool to draw a rectangle that covers the entire area of the reflection. With the Selection tool, select the rectangle. Now, in the Color Mixer, choose Linear for the Type to create a basic black-to-white gradient.

Select the white color pointer and reduce its Alpha value to 0 **A**. Then select the black color pointer and set its Alpha value to about 75% **B**. Let's also move the white color pointer over to about midpoint to shift the transition **C**.

Currently the gradient moves from left to right. We want it to be from top to bottom, so the reflection fades as it moves farther from the original. Select the Gradient Transform tool.

First, let's shrink the gradient. Drag the arrow on the right edge in to change the transition **D**.

Then, rotate the gradient 90 degrees: drag the circle at the top, which turns into four circling arrows so that the gradient moves from top to bottom **E**, and then drag the arrow down to include the full image in the gradient. Lastly, press F8 to convert the gradient into a movie clip called Mask.

> ### T I P
>
> **More advanced with ActionScript.**
> You can create a reflection by using
> the new BitmapData object. This is
> more advanced than the method
> shown here. Look at the online help
> and read about BitmapData.

> ### T I P
>
> **Blending Modes.** We'll apply a
> transparency gradient mask to the
> reflection, but you may also want
> to apply the Multiply blending mode
> to the reflection for good measure.
> select the Reflection layer, select the
> reflection, and then apply the blend-
> ing mode in the Properties inspector.

> ### T I P
>
> **Fine-tuning.** We're flying a little blind
> on this one, because the effect won't
> appear until we've applied Action-
> Script. But you can fine-tune the gradi-
> ent settings at any time. Just select
> the Mask layer and double-click the
> mask. Then make the adjustments.

3. Prepare for Scripting

Masks with transparency don't work
the way other masks do. In order for the
transparency gradient to take effect, we
need to add some simple ActionScript.
In order to add the ActionScript, we first
need to name the instances.

Select the mask with the Selection tool,
and then open the Properties Inspector.
Name the instance mask. Select Use
Runtime Bitmap Caching, too. The transparency mask requires runtime bitmap
caching to work. Lock the Mask layer.

Now, do the same with the reflection.
Unlock and select the Reflection layer.
Select the reflection itself, and name
the instance reflection. Select Runtime
Bitmap Caching there, too. We're ready
to script now.

4. Add ActionScript

We'll add a line of very simple Action-
Script to set the mask. With layer 1 of
the Reflection layer selected, open the
Actions panel. We won't need Script
Assist, so turn it off.

Type

```
reflection.setMask(mask);
```

We're targeting the instance named
Reflection, using the setMask command
to set the Mask, and in parentheses,
specifying the mask movie clip instance
to serve as the mask.

Press Ctrl+Enter (Windows) or
Cmd+Return (Mac OS) to test the project.
The reflection should fade nicely. 🖱

Importing 3D Animation

Import animation from 3D applications as image sequences that you can modify for your Flash file.

**Michael Donnellan
Red-Scorpion.com**

1. Import the Image Sequence

If you've created animation in 3D software, you can export it from that application as an image sequence that Flash will recognize. For this lesson, we're using a 3D animation that my friend, Michael Donnellan from RedScorpion.com, made using Maya software and exported as an image sequence.

We'll add it to a Flash project to create an exciting introduction to a tire company's website. Open the 3D_start.fla file from the How to Wow CD.

Michael has included all the layers in a movie clip, so the stage is just a black object when you first open the file. Double-click on the little circle in the upper-left corner of the stage to open the movie clip symbol, Symbol 2, which contains the timeline we need to work with.

If you scrub through the timeline, you can see the graphics and text that have already been animated for this project.

The text was also created in a 3D application and imported as an image sequence.

Now, let's import the image sequence we're going to be working with. Select the first frame in the Image Seq layer. Then choose File > Import > Import to Stage. Navigate to the Chapter 4: 3D Sequence folder, which contains 76 images. Select the first image, and click Open. Flash will alert you that the image is part of a sequence, and ask whether to import all the images in the sequence. Click Yes.

Flash imports the images, each in its own keyframe. It may take a few minutes to import all the images. When it's done, you'll see a wheel on the stage. If you scrub through the timeline, you'll see the full image sequence. Each keyframe holds an individual image, but if you scrub the playhead through it, you can see how it animates.

2. Repeat the Sequence

Scrub through the timeline. The wheel is animated for 75 frames and then stops. But we want it to continue moving as the text appears and animates. So we'll repeat the sequence. We could import all the keyframes again, but that would greatly increase the file size. Instead, we'll reuse the imported files.

First, remove the extra frames from the Image Seq layer. Select all the frames after frame 76 and then press Shift+F5 to remove them. Then select all the keyframes in frames 1 through 76: select frame 1, hold down the Shift key, and select frame 76. Right-click (Windows) or Control-click (Mac OS) and choose Copy Frames. After Flash has finished copying the frames, select frame 77, right-click, and choose Paste Frames.

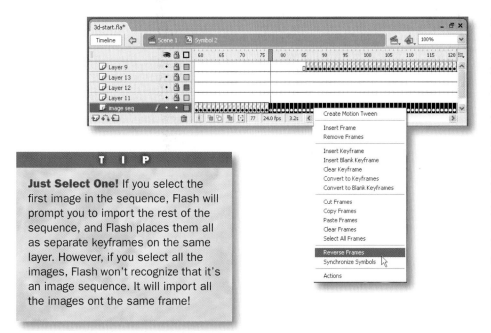

3. Reverse the Frames

The sequence is twice as long now, but if you scrub through the timeline, you'll notice that there is an abrupt change from frame 76 to frame 77. We need to reverse the order of the frames we just pasted so that the animation moves smoothly.

Select frames 77 through the last keyframe. Right-click (Windows) or Control-click (Mac OS) and choose Reverse Frames.

Now, scrub the timeline through frames 75 through 80. It's better, certainly, but there are two frames that are exactly the same, right at the transition. To remove one, select frame 77 and press Shift+F6 to clear the keyframe, and then press Shift+F5 to remove the frame.

TIP

Just Select One! If you select the first image in the sequence, Flash will prompt you to import the rest of the sequence, and Flash places them all as separate keyframes on the same layer. However, if you select all the images, Flash won't recognize that it's an image sequence. It will import all the images ont the same frame!

4. Extend the Sequence

The animation is working well, but it ends too soon. Let's repeat the whole sequence again. Select the first keyframe through the last in the Image Seq layer, and copy the frames. Then, select the first frame after the last keyframe, and paste the frames.

Now take a look at the transition point from one sequence to the other. This time, there are three identical keyframes. Use Shift+F6 and Shift +F5 to remove two of them.

There are still 13 frames that have content on other layers, but not on the Image Seq layer. We'll move the entire sequence down by adding frames at the beginning. Select the first keyframe on the Image Seq layer, and press F5 13 times to add thirteen frames. The animation will be the same length, but it will start 13 frames later.

5. Animate the Opacity

Now, the tire appears and just sits there until the animation begins at frame 14. Let's make that a little more interesting by changing the opacity so that the tire gradually appears. First, we need to convert it to a movie clip symbol, so select the tire and then press F8. Then create a keyframe at frame 14, and create a motion tween between frames 1 and 13. Select the first frame, select the symbol on the stage, and open the Properties Inspector. Choose Alpha from the Color menu, and set it to 0%.

Press Ctrl+Enter (Windows) or Cmd+Return (Mac OS) to test the animation. The wheel gradually appears, begins moving, continues moving as the text moves in, stays, and then disappears. That's a pretty effective introduction to a website!

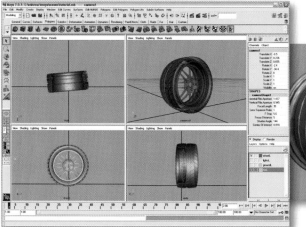

Rendering for Flash in 3D. There are many different 3D applications such as Maya, 3D Studio Max, Cinema 4D, Strata 3D, Lightwave and others. Some are even freeware or open-source (translation, free) such as Blender or Wings 3D.

Most 3D applications share the basic concepts. The render settings shown here are for Maya, but you can adapt them for whatever 3D application you choose.

Notice the format chosen was Windows Bitmap, this is fine for Windows, otherwise I would recommend .png, .jpg or .tif. See that the start frame is frame 1 and the end frame is 96, this will make sure that the animation sequence is exported and not just the current frame.

Make sure that you choose your final imagesize to match as closely as you can to the Flash stage size.

We have included a walkthrough of the 3D creation process as a PDF on the CD.

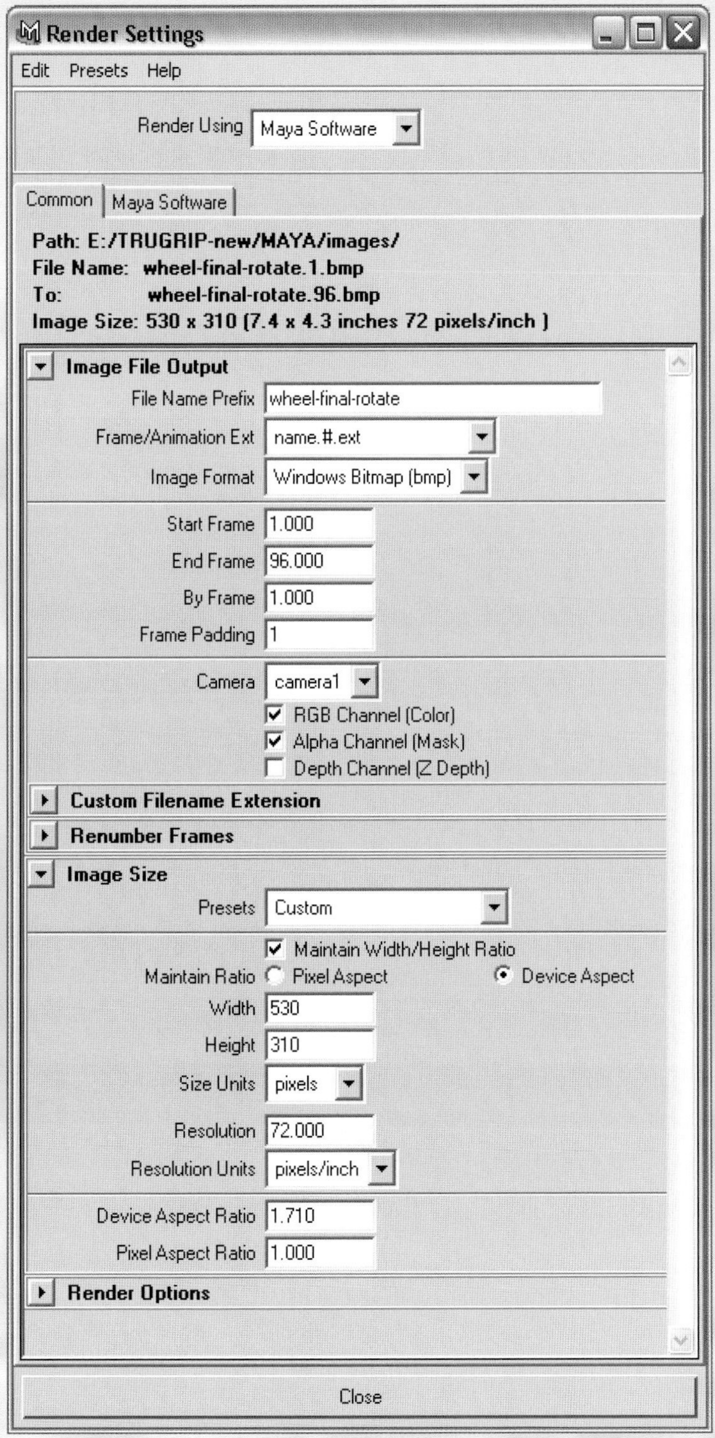

Render Settings

Edit   Presets   Help

Render Using   Maya Software ▼

Common | Maya Software

Path: E:/TRUGRIP-new/MAYA/images/
File Name: wheel-final-rotate.1.bmp
To: wheel-final-rotate.96.bmp
Image Size: 530 x 310 (7.4 x 4.3 inches 72 pixels/inch)

▼ **Image File Output**

File Name Prefix   wheel-final-rotate
Frame/Animation Ext   name.#.ext ▼
Image Format   Windows Bitmap (bmp) ▼

Start Frame   1.000
End Frame   96.000
By Frame   1.000
Frame Padding   1

Camera   camera1 ▼
☑ RGB Channel (Color)
☑ Alpha Channel (Mask)
☐ Depth Channel (Z Depth)

▶ **Custom Filename Extension**

▶ **Renumber Frames**

▼ **Image Size**

Presets   Custom ▼

☑ Maintain Width/Height Ratio
Maintain Ratio ○ Pixel Aspect   ● Device Aspect
Width   530
Height   310
Size Units   pixels ▼

Resolution   72.000
Resolution Units   pixels/inch ▼

Device Aspect Ratio   1.710
Pixel Aspect Ratio   1.000

▶ **Render Options**

Close

5

CHARACTER ANIMATION

Chris Georgenes (mudbubble.com) reveals his secrets to creating life-like character animations.

HINGING ANIMATION *110*

DISTRIBUTE TO LAYERS *111*

WALK CYCLES *112*

ANTICIPATION *117*

LIP SYNC *118*

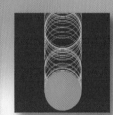

EASING TWEENS *120*

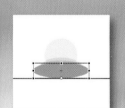

SQUASH AND STRETCH *122*

SELECTIVE ANIMATION *125*

FORM FOLLOWS FUNCTION *127*

I AM NOT AN ANIMATOR. I don't know what it feels like to work with a light table or even a 35mm camera, and I'll never hand-paint thousands of cels. I have an immeasurable respect for traditional animators and the massive amount of love, labor, and commitment they must possess to produce traditionally animated films, but there will always be a disconnect between me and the world of traditional animation. I take this moment to thank traditional animators everywhere for having such long coattails for artists like me to ride on.

About now, you're probably asking "So, why are you writing about animation?"

I am a digital animator. I learned how to animate on a computer. I'll admit to borrowing certain techniques traditionalists have invented, but ultimately, any animation program can have a mechanical feel to it since we work by selecting options from menus much of the time. The trick I have learned is how to make a software program like Flash feel more organic, as if it were a ball of clay. If this book teaches you anything, I hope it teaches you to think differently as to how you approach Flash. Just because the help docs, online resources, or even other books tell you how something can or should be done, don't take that as carved in stone. Take it as carved in clay; you can continue to expand upon the ways the tools are used, beyond what you've read or seen. One hundred people given balls of clay would each create something unique because of the organic nature of the medium. Clay can be pushed and pulled in any diretion, and this is how I encourage you to approach Flash as well.

Many years before Flash existed, I received my B.F.A. from the Hartford Art School (Connecticut). I studied everything from art history to sculpture, color theory to lithography, and above all, how to draw. The progression to the world of computer graphics and animation wasn't difficult. I feel just as comfortable with a mouse or stylus in my hand as I do with pencil, paintbrush, airbrush, or printing press. They are all just tools, each as powerful as the other. A quick and loosely sketched pencil drawing can have just as much impact visually as a full-blown animated action sequence that took 3 months to complete. It's the subject matter that counts.

I've been asked why I share my home-grown tips and techniques, and why I'm not afraid that others will emulate my personal style. Remember that ball of clay? Everyone is different, so all people express themselves uniquely, whether it's through a ball of clay or an animation program like Flash. These are just tools, and in different hands come unique results. I'll show you how I use these tools for my own self-expression. Your own results may, and probably will, vary.

I have spent several years adapting and inventing Flash drawing and animation techniques. This book will show you different ways of approaching Flash and how to make it work for you. Whenever possible, I avoid explaining what is readily available in the help docs and the multitude of online resources. You bought this book to learn what isn't found anywhere else. You will get a firsthand look at how I create characters and motion graphics from scratch, and learn how Flash, as a tool, can be pushed and pulled, limited only by your imagination.

My philosophy, with tools like Flash, is to learn as much as I can, then go back to the first 10 percent of what I learned, and take a left turn. Enjoy the journey.

Chris Georgenes – mudbubble.com

Hinging Animation

Place hinges where they'd naturally occur to efficiently animate a character's body parts.

Move the Transformation Point

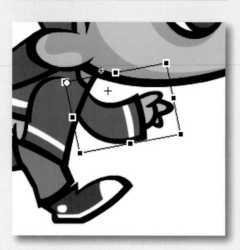

The transformation point is the point around which Flash rotates an object. When you're animating characters, the transformation point should be at the joint where two body parts connect, such as the shoulder or the knee.

To position the transformation point, first select the Free Transform tool and then click the body part symbol on the stage. The transformation point (a solid white circle) is initially aligned with the center point of the symbol. Drag it to the position from which the body part would rotate. For example, if you plan to swing your character's arm, move the transformation point for the upper arm to the shoulder; likewise, move the transformation point for the lower arm to the elbow.

Once you've moved the transformation point for a symbol, it remains in that position until you move it again. That's great because you'd rarely want to pivot a body part from its center!

Animate the Symbol

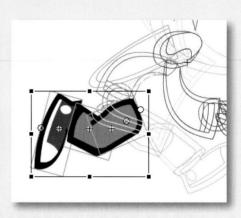

Using the Free Transform tool, rotate the symbol to animate it. The symbol rotates from the transformation point, so it's easier to achieve a more natural movement. You can animate the symbol as you would any other, creating keyframes and applying motion tweens to create smooth movement. ▥

Distribute to Layers

Don't waste hours by copying symbols to layers and renaming each one; this tip will make it easy.

Layers Made Easy

Motion tweening animation requires objects to be on different layers. Copying and pasting each object onto its own layer is a tedious chore, but you can perform the same task with the Distribute to Layers command. Select all the objects you need to distribute, whether they're currently on the same layer or multiple layers. You can distribute any type of element on the stage, including graphic objects, instances, bitmaps, video clips, and broken-apart text blocks. When they're all selected, right-click them, and choose Distribute to Layers. Flash moves each object to its own new, separate layer, and it names the layer for the object. (Layers for graphic objects that don't have names are named Layer 1, Layer 2, and so on.) You can safely delete any layers that are now empty.

CHRIS GEORGENES

Walk Cycles

Almost every character has to walk at some point. Keyframes and a little know-how can get your character across the stage gracefully.

1. Take a Walk

Animation imitates life. To see how the body moves while walking, take a stroll. Notice that your right leg and left arm swing forward together, and so do your left leg and right arm. Pay attention to the length of your stride, the position of your foot, how your foot leaves the ground, and how it returns. Walk the way your character would walk, whether the character bounces happily or shuffles its feet.

2. Prepare Your Character to Walk

Animating a walk cycle is easiest if you design your character in 3/4 view. Create each section of the character as a separate symbol, with the appropriate name. For example, create symbols for the right foot, left foot, right thigh, left thigh, and so on. Then, convert the entire character and all its parts into a graphic or movie clip symbol; we will be working entirely inside this symbol to create our animation.

Convert to Symbol

Name: mudbubble_boy_walk_cycle

Type:
- Movie clip
- Button
- ● Graphic

Registration: ▣

OK
Cancel
Advanced

Press F8 to open the Convert to Symbol dialog box. Name and save the symbol. Right-click (Windows) or Control-click (Mac OS) each symbol. When they are all converted choose Modify > Timeline >Distribute to Layers.

The best way to create a walk cycle in Flash is to animate the character walking in place, as if on a conveyor belt, creating the entire walk cycle within the symbol. Use just enough frames in the walk cycle to create a seamless looping sequence, anywhere from 3 to 30 frames long, depending on the complexity of the animation. Then, use a motion tween to animate the character walking across the scene.

3. Create the First Leg's Positions

On the movie clip symbol's Timeline work with just one leg first. Determine the major walk positions you want to use. For Mudbubble Boy, I've created four major walk positions: the foot planted firmly on the ground, the leg just before it is lifted off the ground, the leg completely off the ground in its most rearward position, and the leg in its most forward position off the ground. Create a keyframe for each position, and use the Free Transform tool to rotate each leg symbol into the appropriate position.

If you don't have a drawn floor or ground, use a horizontal ruler guide as a reference point to ensure that the foot comes in contact with the ground appropriately. Using a guide can prevent the foot from drifting out of alignment with the rest of the body.

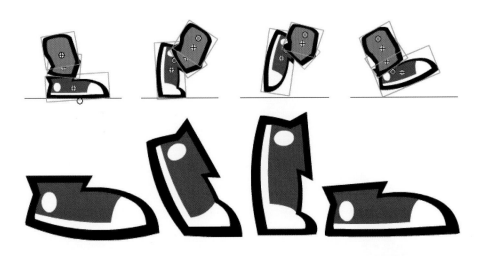

INSIGHT

More Frames Means Slower Movement. The more frames you insert between movements, the slower the animation will be. Experiment with the number of frames between each of your leg positions. To create the illusion that the character is heavy or carrying something heavy, include more frames when the foot is sliding back along the ground, so that movement is slower, and fewer frames while the leg is off the ground, returning it quickly to its initial position. To suggest the character is on a slippery surface, such as ice or a banana peel, include fewer frames when the foot is on the ground and more while it is off the ground.

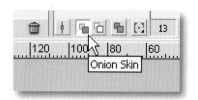

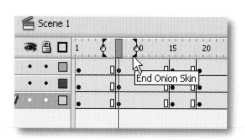

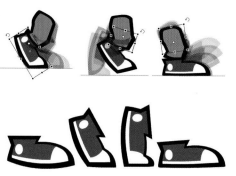

4. Animate the First Leg

When you've created the major leg positions, you can animate the leg. Enable the Onion Skin feature and adjust the Onion Skin brackets to use your established leg positions as references. Then, create new keyframes across all the layers that contain your leg symbols. Use the Free Transform tool to rotate and position each leg symbol into an intermediate position relative to the keyframes you already created.

You could use motion tweening, but you'll have more control over the leg positions if you modify them for each keyframe. Play your animation frequently to get real-time visual feedback on the work you're doing.

TIP

Modify the Symbol. You may want to change the shape of the foot for some of the positions, as I did here. Or, if the character is wearing billowy pants, for example, change the shape of the leg in certain positions. To modify the symbol, duplicate it, give the duplicate a new name, and then edit its shape for the new position.

INSIGHT

Think of the Leg as a Pulley. Sometimes it helps not to think of the leg as a leg, but as a mechanical assembly such as a basic pulley or lever system. The Leg_simulation.fla file on the How to Wow CD is a walk-cycle experiment I made to show how to think of it in mechanical terms.

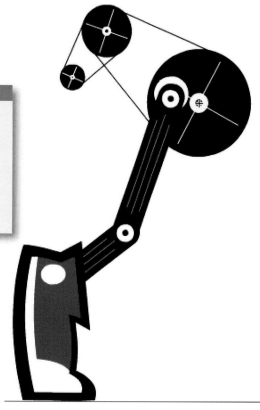

5. Animate the Second Leg

When you're satisfied with the movement of the first leg, move to the second. Unless there's a specific reason that your character's legs might move differently, such as a wooden leg, you can use the work you did on the first leg to move the second.

Delete the second leg entirely from the stage. Then, select all the frames and layers of your leg animation, right-click (Windows) or Control-click (Mac OS), and choose Copy Frames. Create a new layer or select the empty layer that your old leg symbol was in, and right-click (Windows) or Control-click (Mac OS) and choose Paste Frames.

Of course, if you simply use the other leg animation, both legs move at the same time—not a convincing walk. To alternate the legs, select the first half of the frames in the layers you just pasted. Then, drag those frames down the timeline and drop them after the end of the leg animation. Now, select the entire range of frames and drag it to start on frame 1. To delete any residual frames, right-click (Windows) or Control-click (Mac OS) and choose Remove Frames.

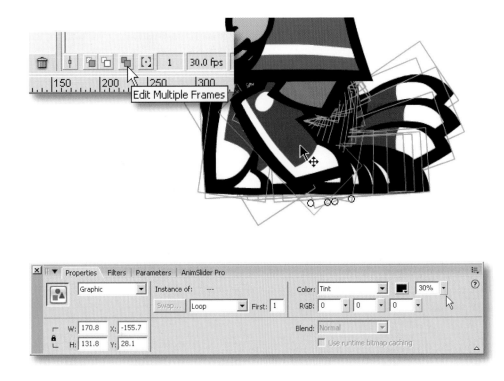

6. Create Depth for the Back Leg

The back leg and front leg shouldn't look identical, because the back leg is further from the viewer. Let's work only with the leg symbols. Lock all layers except those that contain the back leg. Enable Edit Multiple Frames, and then move the Onion Skin markers to include the entire length of the timeline. Click on the stage and choose Edit > Select All. Now, all the symbols for the back leg in all the frames of the animation are selected. Using the Selection tool, click on any of the selected leg symbols to bring them into focus. In the Properties Inspector, choose Tint from the Color menu, select black for the fill color, and set a 30% tint. This gives the illusion that the back leg is in shadow. With Edit Multiple Frames still enabled, nudge the entire back leg animation up and to the right with the arrow keys. This creates some space between the legs and returns the perspective to the original 3/4 view. When you're done, turn off Edit Multiple Frames.

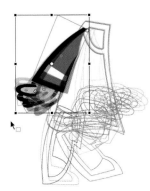

7. Animate the Arms

Animating the arms for a walk cycle is much easier than animating the legs. Arms move relative to the legs, and you can swing them as much as you want to fit your character's personality and mood. You can use frame-by-frame animation, as with the legs, or motion tweens, depending on the complexity of the movement.

As with the legs, animate one of the arms and then copy and paste its frames into a new layer for the second arm, and then shift the animation frames to move the arms alternately. Use the Edit Multiple Frames feature to add the same color tint to the back arm and hand, and use the arrow keys to nudge it into position.

Library - Untitled-1

Untitled-1

24 items

Name	Type	
boy_nose_1	Graphic	
boy_pupil1	Graphic	
boy_sneaker	Graphic	
boy_sneaker 4	Graphic	
boy_sneaker2	Graphic	
boy_sneaker3	Graphic	
boy_upperleg	Graphic	
mudbubble_boy_walkcycle	Graphic	

8. Move the Character Across the Stage.

Because the entire walk cycle was created within a symbol, it's easy to make the character walk across the stage. Return to the stage and then drag an instance of the symbol onto the stage. Create a second keyframe for the end of the scene, and then move the instance to the other side of the stage. Right-click (Windows) or Control-click (Mac OS) on the frames and choose Create Motion Tween.

Play your animation to see the character walk across the stage. You may need to increase or decrease the frames in the tween if the character's feet appear to be slipping, but with some minor adjustments to the number of frames, you should find the appropriate length so that the feet seem to truly grip the surface.

Anticipation

Anticipation builds tension and prepares the viewer—for what is to come.

About Anticipation

By definition, anticipation is the preparation for a particular action or movement. It's useful in animation to attract the viewer's attention to a specific event that is about to occur. For example, an archer pulling an arrow back along a bow anticipates the action of the arrow's release. Likewise, a person bending his knees may anticipate a jump.

How you create anticipation depends on the kind of action you're working with. It may help to perform the task yourself, or watch a movie that includes a similar scene, and keep an eye on the details that precede the action.

A Simple Example

You don't need to have complicated motion to include anticipation. For example, in an animation of a sphere rolling across the stage and filling a box on the other side, I've created anticipation by skewing the ball the opposite direction before it begins to roll. You can see this animation in the ballinbox.fla file included on the How to Wow CD.

Without anticipation, your animation may appear too abrupt and unnatural. It is important as an animator to study from life and notice how we move and react anatomically.

Anticipation in a Character's Actions

The key is to consider what will build tension and inform the viewer that something is about to happen. I've included an example of the same scene with anticipation and without on the How to Wow CD. Open and play cowboy.fla and cowboy_noanticipation.fla. See the difference?

In this example, the cowboy jumps. The scene without anticipation is fine, but adding anticipation makes it more likely that the viewer will notice the jump and understand that it's significant. It's also more believable; in real life, we prepare in subtle ways before we jump, throw, or make other movements.

Create animation in the opposite direction of the jump, and then ease out the movement to imply physical tension. Sometimes an animation requires more than one keyframe position to achieve the right movement and gesture. In this case, I used four different gestures for the anticipation animation, each with a motion tween and some easing applied. ▥

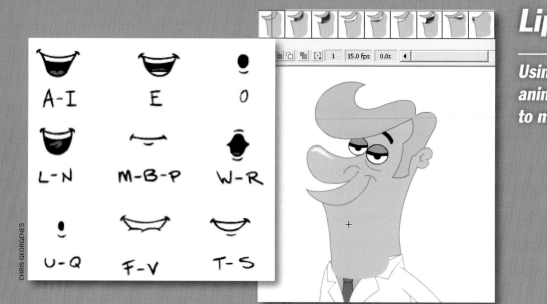

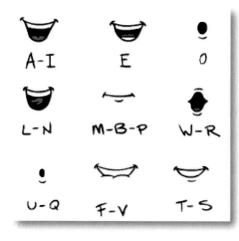

CHRIS GEORGENES

Lip Sync

Using symbols, you can animate characters' mouths to match their speech.

1. Create Mouth Symbols

As we articulate words, our mouths form different shapes. Animations are more compelling when the characters' mouths move in relationship to their speech. We'll need to create several symbols for each character to represent all the likely mouth positions. Draw each of the standard mouth shapes for your character, and then convert each into a symbol in Flash, so that they're all available in the library.

T I P

Naming Mouth Symbols. Name the symbols with the letter sounds they represent so that you can find the symbol easily, without having to think through the mouth position each time or preview each symbol.

▼ Library – lipSync_sample.fla

lipSync_sample.fla

22 items

Name	Type
mouth A-I	Graphic
mouth A-I noTeeth	Graphic
mouth E	Graphic
mouth F-V	Graphic
mouth L-N	Graphic
mouth M-B-P	Graphic
mouth O-ooooh	Graphic
mouth R	Graphic
mouth T-S	Graphic

Customize the Shapes for Your Character. When designing a character, conceptualize how the character's features might work. For example, some mouths are independent of the jaw and nose, while others are an integral part of the other facial features. If changes in the mouth's position will alter the character's other facial features, be sure to include those features in the symbols you create.

2. Nest Mouth Symbols into a Single Multi-Frame Symbol

We have nine symbols to choose from, but they're all based on the same mouth. We'll create a single symbol with each of the mouth shapes on a different frame. Choose Insert > New Symbol, select Graphic for the type, and name it Mouth. Drag the first mouth shape symbol onto the stage. Insert a keyframe for the second frame, delete the first symbol, and drag the second symbol onto the stage. Continue until you've created a separate keyframe for each of the nine Mouth symbols.

3. Apply the Appropriate Mouth Shapes

Return to Scene 1, and place the Mouth symbol in the appropriate place for your character. As you move through the dialogue, click the mouth instance on the stage. Then, in the First field, type the frame number you want to use **A**, and press Enter. For example, if you want to use the second mouth shape, type 2 and press Enter. Flash substitutes the frame you specify.

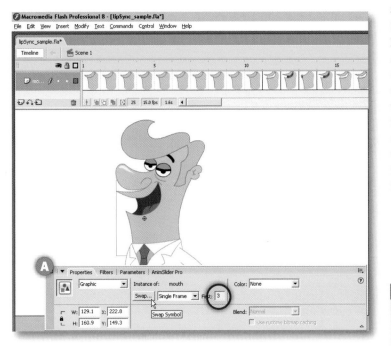

Changing Timeline Views. You can see which shape is assigned to each frame in the timeline. Choose Preview from the Timeline drop-down menu to see the image in each frame. This menu includes other commands to change the appearance of the Timeline as well.

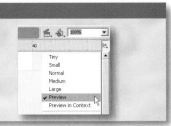

Swap Symbols Method. I've shown you the method I prefer to use, because it's faster and easier to use for long dialogues. However, you can also swap symbols in the timeline. Create a keyframe where you need to change symbols, select the Mouth symbol on the stage, and then click Swap in the Properties Inspector. In the Swap Symbols dialog box, select the new symbol and click OK.

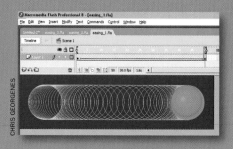

CHRIS GEORGENES

Easing Tweens

By default, motion tweens create animations that move at a consistent speed. Easing gradually increases or decreases the movement over time, creating a more natural effect.

About Easing

Apply easing to gradually accelerate or decelerate the movement in a tween. Easing is useful for creating the illusion of gravity and weight. For example, a ball tossed into the air gradually slows as it ascends (easing out), and then its speed increases as it falls back to Earth (easing in). You can also use easing to dramatize the approach of a character, increase the momentum of a train or airplane, or vary a character's gait.

Flash tweens the motion so that the change occurs consistently across the targeted frames. To apply standard easing, select any tweened frame in the Timeline, and then choose a value from the Ease menu **A** in the Properties Inspector. Positive values cause the motion to decelerate, and negative values cause it to accelerate.

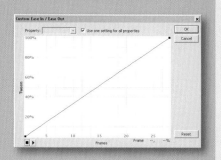

Customizing the Ease

When the standard easing settings don't provide the effect you want, customize the ease settings. Click Edit **B** next to the Ease field in the Properties Inspector to open the Custom Ease In/Ease Out dialog box.

The graph in the dialog box represents the degree of motion over time.

The horizontal axis represents the frames, and the vertical axis represents the percentage of change to the object. The curve in the graph determines the rate of change. When the curve is horizontal (no slope), the object doesn't move until the final keyframe; when the curve is vertical (no slope), the object moves right away and then remains static until the final keyframe.

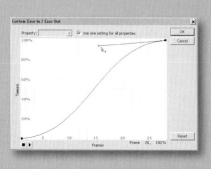

Click the curve to add a new control point, and then drag it to a new position. Below the graph, Flash displays the coordinates of the point: the frame number and the percentage of change. Control points include tangent points (hollow squares); use these to change the angle of the curve.

To see the effect of your changes, click the Play button in the lower-left corner. Flash previews the animation on the stage using the current curve.

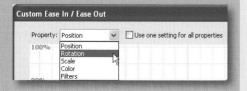

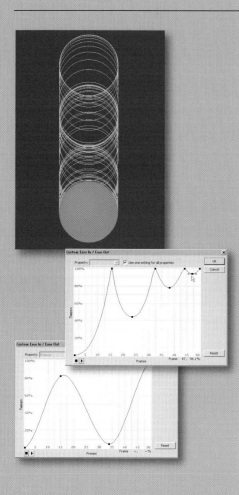

Working with Different Properties

Tweening can affect an object's position, rotation, scale, color, or filters, and you can ease each property separately. By default, Use One Setting for All Properties is selected, and all tweened properties change at the same rate.

Position: Affects the position of an animated object on the stage.

Rotation: Affects the rotation settings. For example, you can fine-tune how quickly an animated character turns around to face the user on the stage.

Scale: Affects the rate at which an object resizes. For example, you may want to adjust the speed of scaling so that an object appears to move away from the viewer, then comes closer, and then moves away again.

Color: Affects the rate of color transitions.

Filters: Affects the rate of change in filter settings. For example, you can adjust the ease setting of a drop shadow that simulates a change in the direction of a light source, such as the sun.

Experiment!

I've included sample files on the How to Wow CD so that you can get a feel for the advanced easing options. Easing_2.fla is an animation of a ball falling and bouncing until it comes to a resting position. You can adjust the ease to simulate gravity's effect on the ball's trajectory so that the bouncing mimics the behavior of a real ball. This entire animation is just two keyframes and a motion tween, with custom easing controlling all of the changes. Create keyframes for the ball at its highest point and its resting position, create a motion tween, and then modify the easing to create every other position.

To create the first bounce, add a point around frame 15, and drag this point to the top of the graph so the tween is at 100%. Make sure the handles are close to the point to reduce the amount of easing when the ball bounces back up. Then, add another point at approximately frame 25 with a tween of 50%. This time, adjust the handles so that the curve is rounded; the more gradual the curve, the more the ball will ease out. Add more points to the curve, reducing the amount of tween with each one and increasing the amount of easing.

Easing_3.fla is an animation of a ball scaling from small to large. Open the Custom Ease In/Ease Out dialog box to see the curve, which goes up and down and back up. 🖮

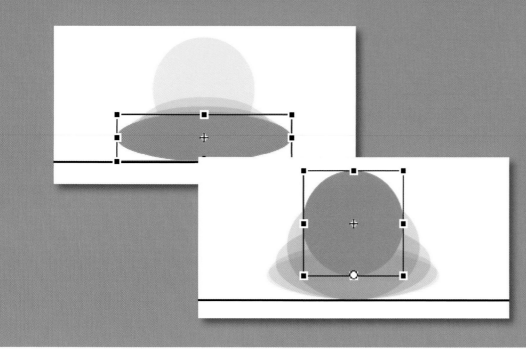

Squash & Stretch

Liven up your animations with objects that squash and stretch on impact.

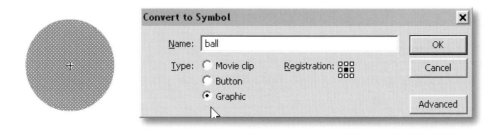

1. Create a Simple Animation

Squash and stretch is a traditional animation technique for adding realism and weight to objects. When a moving object comes into contact with a stationary object, it deforms a bit, depending on its flexibility. Traditional animation exaggerates this effect, and that's what we'll do here.

We'll work with a bouncing ball, though you can use this technique with any objects. Draw a circle and press F8 to convert it to a graphic symbol. Create a keyframe at about frame 20. Select the symbol on the stage, and then hold down the Shift key while you nudge it down using the arrow keys. Let the ball hover just above the landing area. Then, right-click anywhere between the keyframes, and choose Create Motion Tween.

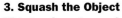

2. Ease the Object In

A ball thrown into the air won't fall back down at a consistent speed; it will accelerate as it descends. Select frame 1. In the Properties Inspector, set the Ease value to −100. The ball will fall slower at first, with its speed gradually increasing.

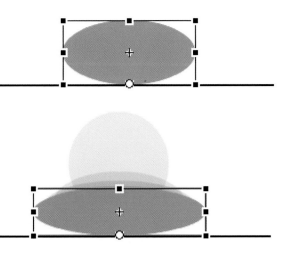

3. Squash the Object

This is where it gets fun. Let's make the ball partially flatten when it hits the ground. Create a keyframe a few frames after the second keyframe. Select the ball on stage. With the Free Transform tool, move the transformation point to the very bottom of the ball. Then, use the handles on the sides to stretch the ball and the handle on the top to push it down. Nudge the ball so that its bottom edge is touching the landing surface.

Create additional keyframes, flattening the ball further.

4. Stretch the Object

As the ball bounces up, it stretches. I like to exaggerate this frame, emphasizing the springing effect of the ball launching from the ground. Create another keyframe and use the Free Transform tool to stretch the ball so that it is tall and thin.

5. Complete the Animation

We're done squashing and stretching. To finish this animation, right-click frame 1 and choose Copy Frames. Then, right-click a frame a few frames after the last keyframe and choose Paste Frames. The ball will return to its original position and size, so that the animation can loop seamlessly.

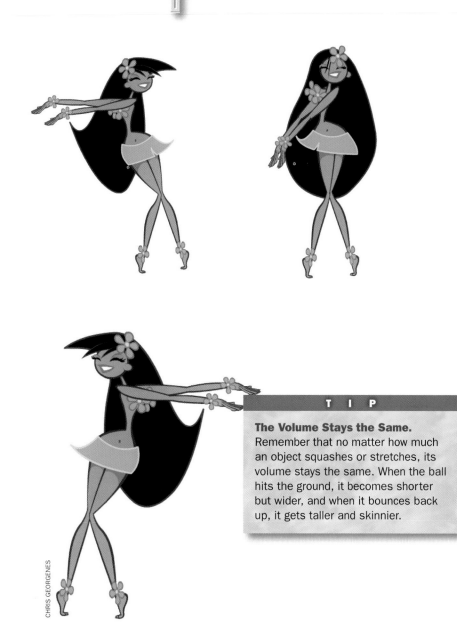

CHRIS GEORGENES

Right-click between the last two keyframes, and choose Create Motion Tween. Select the second-to-last keyframe. In the Properties Inspector, set the Ease value to 100 to ease the ball out as it bounces up.

Press Ctrl+Enter (Windows) or Cmd+Return (Mac OS) to survey your handiwork and watch a ball bounce, squashing and stretching as it hits the ground and returns back up.

Of course, this technique is useful for animations that don't include balls, too. Watch how objects interact with other objects or space around them, and then use those observations in your animation. For example, you can use this technique to exaggerate the impact of a thrown newspaper slamming into a rosebush, or the way a hula girl's hair expands and flattens as she dances.

> **TIP**
>
> **Frame Rate.** I'm using a frame rate of 24 fps, a standard speed, because I work with this rate often and know how many frames it will take to make something move at a certain speed at this rate. 24 fps is fast enough for relatively smooth animation without pushing the limits of most computers.

> **TIP**
>
> **The Volume Stays the Same.** Remember that no matter how much an object squashes or stretches, its volume stays the same. When the ball hits the ground, it becomes shorter but wider, and when it bounces back up, it gets taller and skinnier.

CHRIS GEORGENES

Selective Animation

Sometimes it's what you don't see that makes the difference. Blurring and stretching objects on specific frames can turn a good animation into a great one.

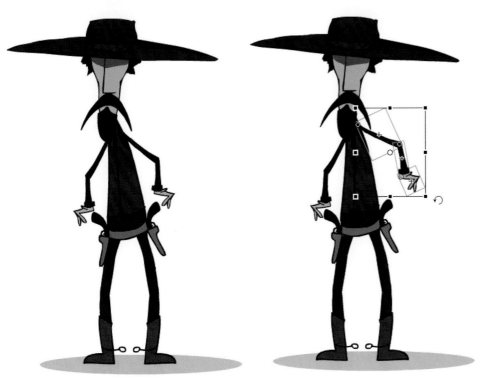

1. Add Anticipation

When you want to draw attention to an action, add anticipation. In the cowboy.fla file on the How to Wow CD, I rotated the arm in a position that suggests the cowboy is about to grab something, and then wiggled his fingers to build the anticipation even more. How you add anticipation to a scene depends on the action that's about to take place and how you want your viewer to experience it.

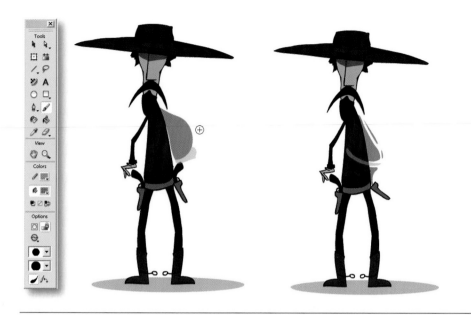

2. Replace the Objects

To smooth movement, replace the objects that will be moving (such as the cowboy's arm) with simple shapes. Create a keyframe at the beginning of the action. For that frame, delete the original object, and draw simple shapes in the appropriate position. Use colors that suggest the objects you're replacing, and mix in some transparency. It's effective to use about 30% transparency, so the background can be seen through the shapes.

Create another keyframe, and draw objects in a different position, still with colors and transparency that suggest the original object.

3. Return to the Objects

Two frames of blurring is just about right for the viewer to get the feeling of movement but not notice the substitution of the object. Create a third keyframe, with the original object in a new position, ready to resume action. In the cowboy scene, I also added some brush strokes behind the arm to suggest that it is still moving but decelerating. Be creative, and remember that the subtle touches make all the difference. ▥

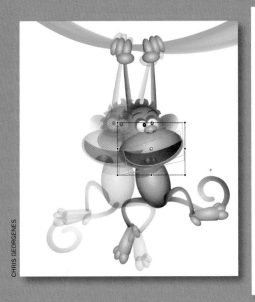

CHRIS GEORGENES

Form Follows Function: Creating 2.5D

Create the illusion of a three-dimensional character while remaining in the two-dimensional world of Flash.

1. Design the Character Symbols

To create a three-dimensional effect, every symbol must be fully independent. Start by designing your character symbols in a 3/4 view on frame 1. Place each symbol on its own layer so that each object can move independently, and so that you can apply motion tweens effectively.

2. Create Initial Keyframes

Create the keyframes where you want the character's head to start and stop turning. In a looping animation, the first frame and last frame must match to ensure continuity. To create the keyframes, select all the layers in the initial frame and then press F6; then, select all the layers in the frame where the head should stop turning and press F6.

3. Plan the Effect

Key to this technique is an understanding of how objects move in space. Think about how the eyes, nose, and other objects would appear if mapped to a rotating sphere, which is basically what a turning head is. When a head rotates, an eye gets bigger as it moves toward you and smaller as it moves away. You may find it helpful to draw sketches of the rotating head, or to actually create a physical model to observe.

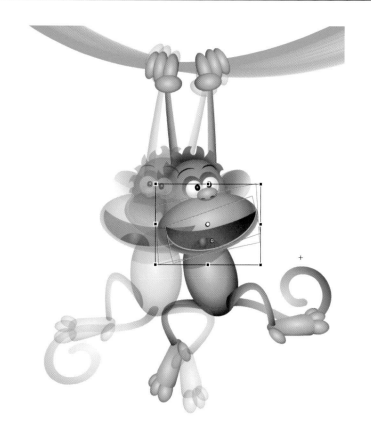

4. Create the Opposite View

Create a keyframe between the two other keyframes. Select the middle keyframe and, applying what you know about perspective, adjust each part of the character for the opposite 3/4 view. The position of each object should be changed to imply a different perspective. Use the Free Transform tool to shape each symbol. This can be tricky, and you won't know exactly how it will look until you apply the motion tweens. You may need to make several adjustments to your symbols throughout this process. It may help to turn on Onion Skin so you can refer to your character's appearance in the first frame as you work.

No matter how tempting it may seem, don't flip your character horizontally to achieve the new view. Once the motion tweens are applied, the symbols will warp and skew in an undesirable way.

5. Create Motion Tweens.

Apply a motion tween to all layers between each set of keyframes, and then play back your animation. You may need to fine-tune the symbols' positions to achieve the illusion of a three-dimensional character. Scrub the Timeline and make adjustments to symbols wherever something doesn't look quite right. How many adjustments you need to make depends on your own level of perfectionism as well as the complexity of your character. ▥

T I P

Remember Travel Speed. To make this animation look convincingly three-dimensional, make sure that closer objects move faster and travel a greater distance than objects farther away. Therefore, in the example, the amount of rotation and repositioning of the monkey's mouth is more exaggerated than his hair and ears.

T I P

Less Is More. Don't exaggerate the three-dimensional illusion. This effect is best executed with many subtle movements rather than a few major changes.

6

ADDING INTERACTIVITY

Allowing the user to interact with your project engages the user and lets them "touch" your project.

ACTIONSCRIPT *132*

CREATING ADVANCED BUTTONS *134*

CUSTOM ANIMATED PRELOADERS *140*

CUSTOM MOUSE CURSOR *146*

CLICK AND DRAG A MOVIE CLIP *148*

CREATE A DYNAMIC IMAGE GALLERY *152*

WHEN THE WEB WAS YOUNG, and web design was first emerging (not that long ago), just about the only ways to make a page interesting were to add scrolling marquee text or to make it (shudder) blink. I am proud to say that I have never used the <blink> tag, but the limitations were certainly frustrating.

Then, suddenly, there was an explosion of technology. Java and Shockwave, though slow and clumsy, let designers create pages that site visitors could interact with. No longer were visitors simply viewers—now they were participants!

We've come a long way in a short time. With greater bandwidth, and faster download speeds, more exciting interactivity is possible. Flash lets you take advantage of the improvements with many opportunities for getting viewers involved in multimedia projects. Whether developing in Flash for the web or a CD-ROM, you can make so many things touchable.

What you will learn in this chapter will forever change your projects from content people look at to pages people engage with. For example, you've probably seen preloaders that make you envious, far more informative than boring status bars. You'll learn here how to animate your own creative preloaders to keep your viewers interested.

You'll learn how to create smooth, organic buttons that work with your design instead of fighting it. And I'll let you in on the reason many professional Flash designers think movie clip symbols are the answer for most buttons, not button symbols.

Sick of that arrow floating around the page. You can create your own custom cursor, using any image you like, and even animate it. This is the kind of trick that can bring great character to a project—and can easily be overdone. Please use it responsibly.

COLIN SMITH

One of the coolest things you can do is to create a movie clip that your viewers can drag. Dragging something around on the page is sure to bring smiles to faces—yours and your viewers'. I'll show you how to create a spotlight that viewers can drag to light up different areas of the scene. Now that's interactivity!

Finally, we will wrap up a project we began way back in Chapter 2. You will create an image gallery that dynamically loads images from the library and displays them. Click a thumbnail, and the full image appears in all its glory. This is a really fast way to build a gallery of images you can display to a hungry audience.

The Flash techniques in this chapter require a bit more ActionScript than you've used in previous chapters. I've kept scripting to a minimum, and used the simplest scripting possible to get the job done. But by now you've probably realized that to build truly engaging projects, you'll want to learn at least the basics of ActionScript. This is not a book about ActionScript, and we can't cover it all in these pages, so I encourage you to check out some of the fantastic books dedicated to the subject. Meanwhile, I've provided all the scripts you need to unleash your creativity with some great interactive projects.

COLIN SMITH

ActionScript

Go beyond motion tweens and default rollover states. ActionScript lets you get much more creative with your Flash project—without requiring you to become a programmer.

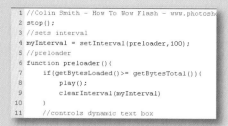

About ActionScript

ActionScript, similar to JavaScript, extends the functionality of Flash dramatically. You can use it for simple tasks such as to attach behaviors to buttons, control movie clips, and timelines all the way to building complex applications that interact with databases.

Some lessons in this book contain ActionScript. I explain the scripting in the context of the lesson, but ActionScript is far too complex to cover thoroughly in this book. Luckily, you don't need to know much ActionScript to take advantage of it. All the examples are on the CD with the completed script ready for your use.

Advancing Your Learning

If you really want to learn ActionScript, there are volumes of wonderful books available to help you. One of my favorites is *Foundation ActionScript,* by Sham Bhangal, which is a great book to get started with. I also recommend books by Colin Mook and Phil Kerman, as well as Macromedia's Training from the Source series. There are tons of useful websites such as actionscript.org or flashkit.com. Don't forget that ActionScript resources are available in Flash itself. Choose Help > Flash Help. Also check out the LiveDocs, which are updated online.

Frame-Based Scripting

In early versions of Flash, all ActionScript was attached to movie clips. That made it difficult to find all the ActionScript in a project, and it could be challenging to control. You can still attach ActionScript to movie clips, but I recommend creating an Actions layer as the top layer in any file that contains ActionScript, and then attaching most of your scripts to frame 1 of that layer. That way, all your scripts are easy to find when you need to make changes, or when someone else needs to work on the project. Of course, as you'll see in some of the lessons in this book, there are exceptions. Sometimes you'll need to create a stop action in a specific frame, for example.

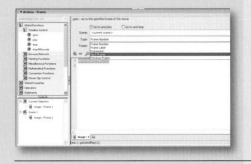

Using Script Assist

You can type the script into the Actions panel, or you can use Script Assist to write the syntax for you. To use it, click Script Assist. Flash divides the Actions panel into sections. Click the Plus sign and choose the script from the library. Flash will write the default code and display fields you can use to customize it.

Even if you don't click the Script Assist button, you can still access the libraries on the left side of the Actions panel.

Scripting Syntax

If you haven't done much scripting, all the parentheses and brackets may seem mysterious and arbitrary. Scripts will seem much more straightforward to you if you learn the following syntax rules:

```
name.event = function(argument){
    perform actions here;
}
```

Use a dot (period) after the instance name you're targeting. This is called dot notation. After the dot comes the command to do something or an event such as a mouse rolling over. Always precede a function with a set of parentheses () and a left bracket, then write the entire function, and close with a right bracket. You can put additional instructions inside the brakets; there are called arguments. For example:

```
colin.writeBook(HTW-Flash){
    HTW-Flash.writebookAndPrint;
}
```

Whenever you are declaring a string (text) use the quotation marks ("") so Flash knows it's not a script.

Always close parentheses and brackets. As in English, you should never have an open parenthesis without a close parenthesis somewhere later in the script.

Use a semicolon to indicate the end of a statement.

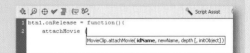

Code Hints

Flash makes it easier for you to write ActionScripts by including code hints. For example, as you type the open parenthesis after an action, such as attachMovie, Flash tells you which information you need to provide for that action. In this case, we need an idName, newName, and depth. (Optional information is shown in brackets.)

COLIN SMITH

Creating Advanced Buttons

Using movie clip symbols and ActionScript, you can create much more sophisticated rollover effects for buttons.

1. Prepare the Button

Instead of using button symbols to create buttons, we'll animate movie clip symbols. I've opened the button_start.fla file from the How to Wow CD.

This file contains four text labels on the page for buttons: Home, Gallery, Words, and Contact. It also includes a green button shape; this is the shape we'll use to create our buttons. First, move that green button shape up next to the Home label. Then, press F8 to convert it to a movie clip symbol called Buttons.

Double-click the button to edit it. Rename the existing layer Button. Then, create three more layers: Action, Labels, and Animation. The button animation should last 15 frames, so move the mouse to frame 15 on the top layer, click to select, and drag downward to select frame 15 for all four layers, then press F5 to create the frames **A**.

2. Add Frame Labels

Because a movie clip symbol doesn't
include rollover states, we'll need to
create them ourselves. To do so, we'll use
frame labels, which are reference names
for frames.

Select frame 8 in the Labels layer, and
press F6 to create a keyframe. Open the
Properties Inspector. Label the frame
"out." Then, select frame 1, and label it
"in." We've created two references within the button symbol's timeline, which
we'll use to animate rollover states.

3. Create the Gradient

To make these buttons more interesting, we'll create an animation when the
mouse moves over them. Animating a
transparency gradient will let us shift the
gradient as the mouse moves in, and then
again as it moves out.

Select the Animation layer. Draw a
rectangle a little bigger than the
existing button **A**. It can have any fill
color, but should have no stroke. Select
the rectangle, and open the Color Mixer
panel. Change the Fill type to Linear.
A basic black-to-white gradient appears
in the gradient bar **B**. By default, there
are two color pointers. Add a third,
closer to the right side. Then, select
each and move the color bar to white **C**.
Now, set the Alpha values for the outside
pointers to 0 and the middle one to 100
D. The outer edges are transparent, with
a middle section that is opaque.

Select the rectangle, and press F8 to
convert it to a movie clip symbol called
Grad, for gradient.

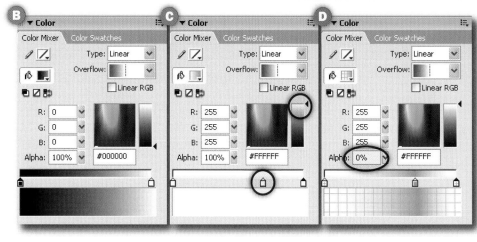

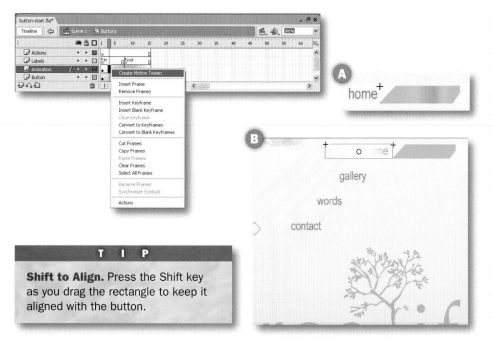

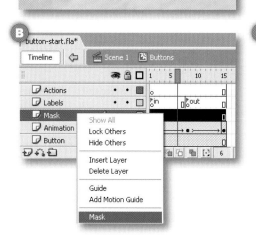

4. Animate the In and Out States

When the mouse moves over the button, the gradient will slide in. To set that up, select frame 8 of the Animation layer, directly beneath the out label. Press F6 to create a keyframe. Then, right-click (Windows) or Control-click (Mac OS) between the keyframes 1 and 8 and choose Create Motion Tween.

Select the first frame in the Animation layer, and move the rectangle to the left of the button. Now create a keyframe on frame 15 of the Animation layer, and create a motion tween between frames 8 and 15. At frame 8, the rectangle is over the button **A**. Select frame 15, and drag the rectangle back to the left so that it will slide off the button as the mouse moves away **B**.

> **TIP**
>
> **Shift to Align.** Press the Shift key as you drag the rectangle to keep it aligned with the button.

> **TIP**
>
> **Editing Symbols.** To edit a symbol, double-click it on the stage or in the Library panel. If you double-click it on the stage, the symbol appears in position, providing context while you edit it. If you double-click it in the library, the symbol opens by itself to fill the screen.

5. Mask the Button

Currently, the gradient affects more than the button as it moves in and out. We need to create a mask to ensure that it only appears on the button itself. We'll start by creating a layer for the mask. Create a new layer. and name it Mask.

Now, we'll copy the button shape. Select the keyframe at frame 1 of the Button layer to select the button, and then press Alt (Windows) or Option (Mac OS) and drag it up to frame 1 of the Mask layer. We should now have a duplicate of the keyframe on the Mask layer **A**.

Drag the Mask layer above the Animation layer. To create the mask, right-click (Windows) or Control-click (Mac OS) the Mask layer and choose Mask **B**. Now, when you scrub through the timeline, the gradient affects only the button **C**.

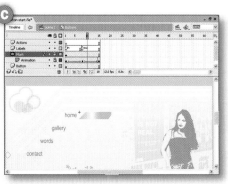

6. Create Stop Actions

The gradient should move in for the in state, but not before the mouse has moved over the button. We'll add a stop action at the beginning so that the animation doesn't start until we want it to. Select the first frame of the Actions layer, open the Actions panel, and type

`stop();`

After the gradient has moved in, it should stop until the mouse moves away from the button. We'll need another stop action. Create a keyframe at frame 7 of the Actions layer, one frame before the out state begins, and add a stop action in the Actions panel.

Now the animation stops until the out state occurs. To make the out state behavior slower, add a couple of frames. Click and hold the Shift key to select a frame between frames 10 and 15 in all five layers, and then press F5 twice to add two frames **A**.

7. Action for the In State

We're ready to create the actions for the rollover states. Return to Scene 1. Move the button over the button Home. In order to target an object with ActionScript, its instance must be named. Select the button, open the Properties Inspector, and name the instance "home." **A**. Now, select the first frame of the Actions layer, and then open the Actions panel and enter

```
home.onRollOver = function(){
    this.gotoAndPlay("in");
}
```

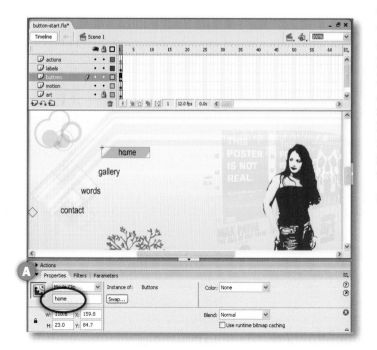

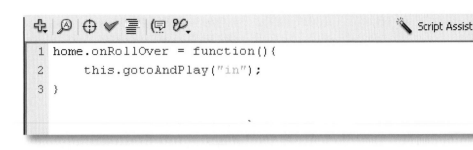

```
1  home.onRollOver = function(){
2      this.gotoAndPlay("in");
3  }
```

The first word is the instance name we're targeting: home. Then we're identifying an event: onRollOver, or when the mouse rolls over the instance. Then we're identifying the function that should happen when the event occurs, in this case an event handler. We want it to go to and play the "in" portion of the movie clip. The keyword this mean that we are targeting the same home movie clip instance that we are currently working in.

To test the action, press Ctrl+Enter (Windows) or Command+Return (Mac OS). Roll over the button. The animation plays, but if you move the mouse off the button, nothing happens, because we haven't scripted anything for the "out" portion of the movie clip.

T I P

Move or Copy. If you just drag a frame to another layer, Flash moves the content, removing it from the original layer. If you press Alt or Option as you drag the frame, Flash copies it to the new layer.

I N S I G H T

Making the Buttons Work. If you have buttons, you want them to do something: take the viewer to a page, play a movie, or any number of things. When you've created the rollover states, you can add to the script to define the button's behavior. Copy the "out" script, substitute onRelease for onRollOut, and then identify the action you want to perform.

```
1  home.onRollOver = function(){
2      this.gotoAndPlay("in");
3  }
4  home.onRollOut = function(){
5      this.gotoAndPlay("out");
6  }
```

8. Write Actions for the Out State

Now we'll script the out state. In the Actions panel, copy the script you typed for the in state, and paste it below. Then, change "onRollOver" to "onRollOut" and change "in" to "out."

Press Ctrl+Enter (Windows) or Cmd+Return (Mac OS) and test the action. Roll over the button, and the gradient moves in; roll off the button, and it moves out. However, if you roll over the button many times, the gradient doesn't quite behave properly.

---

9. Add an Action to Return to the First Frame

To fix the behavior, we need to edit the Buttons symbol. Double-click the button. We've got stop actions on the first and 8th frames of the Actions layer. We need to add an action to the last frame to return to the first frame and wait for another rollover.

```
gotoAndStop(1);
```

Create a keyframe on the last frame of the Actions layer. Open the Actions panel and enter:

```
gotoAndStop(1);
```

Now, when the timeline gets to the last frame, it will return to frame 1 and wait for the next rollover. Return to Scene 1. Test the button; everything should work as expected.

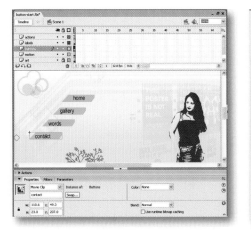

```
home.onRollOver = function(){
    this.gotoAndPlay("in");
}
home.onRollOut = function(){
    this.gotoAndPlay("out");
}


gallery.onRollOver = function(){
    this.gotoAndPlay("in");
}

gallery.onRollOut = function(){
    this.gotoAndPlay("out");
}
```

10. Create Additional Buttons

Once the first button is working properly, it's easy to create additional buttons. Select the button, press the Alt (Windows) or Option (Mac OS) key, and drag out a copy for each of the labels. Then, give each instance a different name: gallery, words, and contact.

Each button needs its own actions, but we can copy most of the script from the first button. Select the first frame of the Actions layer, and open the Actions panel. Then copy the script from the first button and paste it below. In that script, change "home" to "gallery." That's the only change we need to make.

Press Enter or Return a couple of times, and paste the script again, changing the target instance to "words," and then one more time, changing the instance name to "contact." Click the check mark icon to check for errors.

Press Ctrl+Enter (Windows) or Command+Return (Mac OS) to test the rollover effect for all the buttons. Now we have the rollover effect for all of these buttons. To make the buttons lead you to a new page, read Chpter 7.

45%

72%

COLIN SMITH

Custom Animated Preloader

Say goodbye to boring status bars. ActionScript lets you create customized, interesting preloaders.

1. Create Stop Actions

You can use just about any image to create a preloader. For this lesson, we'll animate a logo to fill as the content loads. I've opened the Preloader_start.fla file from the How to Wow CD. There are three layers. The bottom layer, Content, contains the image that may take a few seconds to load. The middle layer, Preloader, will contain the preloader we're about to create. Rename the first layer Actions, and that's where we'll put all the actions.

We need to create a stop action to stop the movie from playing until the preloader allows it to continue. So, select the first frame in the Actions layer, open the Actions panel, and enter

`stop();`

We need another stop action to keep the movie from looping after it's played. So, select frame 2 in the Actions layer, press F6 to create a keyframe, open the Actions panel, and type

`stop();`

2. Create the Preloader Image

The movie will stop and wait for the preloader's instructions, so we'd better create the preloader. Lock the Content layer, so you don't accidentally move it. Then, select the first frame in the Preloader layer. Drag the logo from the library onto the stage, and use the Free Transform tool to scale it up a bit. Drag the registration point, the circle icon, to the bottom, so that the preloader starts filling from the bottom. The logo is a movie clip symbol I created earlier. You will want to create your own logo at some point. In the Properties Inspector, give it an instance name of "logo."

Double-click the logo to edit the symbol. Create two additional layers for the logo. Rename the original layer Logo, the middle layer Mask, and the top layer Outline. We're going to use a mask to fill an outline of the logo as the movie loads. So we need to create an outline. Select the first frame of the Outline layer. Then, select the Ink Bottle tool, set the stroke color to black, and then click on the edge of each of the shapes to color the outlines. Once the outlines are inked, hold down the Shift key and select all of them. Then, choose Edit > Cut. Select the first frame on the Outline layer, and choose Edit > Paste in Place. The outline is now seperated from the fill.

3. Create the Mask

We'll animate a mask to fill the outline while the content loads. We'll create a mask, but we won't animate it on the stage. We'll let the preloader animate it using ActionScript. Lock the Logo and Outline layers.

Select the Rectangle tool with no stroke. Draw a rectangle about the same size as the logo. Select the rectangle, and press F8 to convert it to a movie clip

symbol named "mask." Set the registration point at the bottom. Open the Properties Inspector, and name the instance "mask" **A**.

Finally, create the mask. Right-click the Mask layer and choose Mask **B**.

4. Create the Text Box

We have the outline and the mask, but we want to include a text counter to show the viewer how much of the content has loaded. Let's create the text box. Return to Scene 1. Select the Text tool. Open the Properties Inspector. Choose Dynamic Text from the drop-down menu **A**, and then set up the font, text size, text color, and other attributes. For this lesson, we'll use gray, 14-point _sans text **B**.

Drag the Text tool to create a text box at the bottom of the logo. In the Properties Inspector, name the instance of the text box "myText."

That's all we need to do for the text box for now. The ActionScript will generate the actual text content.

5. Write Script for the Preloader

We've created all the components. Now we need to create the ActionScript that will make the preloader work. Select the first keyframe in the Actions layer, and open the Actions panel. Remember that we created a stop action in this frame earlier. The first stop action keeps Flash from moving to the next frame, where the content is, until everything is loaded. We need to create script that tells Flash when it can move on to the content.

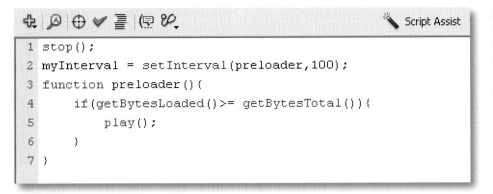

```
1  stop();
2  myInterval = setInterval(preloader,100);
3  function preloader(){
4      if(getBytesLoaded()>= getBytesTotal()){
5          play();
6      }
7  }
```

Script Assist

```
1  stop();
2  myInterval = setInterval(preloader,100);
3  function preloader(){
4      if(getBytesLoaded()>= getBytesTotal()){
5          play();
6          clearInterval(myInterval)
7      }
8  }
```

Script Assist

Here's the basic idea: At specific intervals, we want Flash to check to see whether the content has loaded. If it has, we will progress to the next frame where our content is. If it hasn't, Flash continues to play the preloader until the next time it checks. This is called a condition in ActionScript and makes up a conditional statement. We'll use an interval of 100 milliseconds, so that Flash checks frequently. The first line of script sets up the interval, its name, and frequency. We'll begin defining the preloader function in the next line.

Flash needs some criteria for determining whether the content has loaded. We will use the conditional statement if. We'll have it compare the number of bytes that have loaded with the total number of bytes in the content, and if the loaded number is greater than or equal to the total number, it can play the movie. It determined this by using the => operator. If the condition is true, the script will continue to the next line; otherwise it will loop back to the top.

Write the script on the left and then click the check mark icon to verify that the syntax is correct.

If we test the preloader now, it runs the preloader, the content appears, and then it flashes back to the first frame in a continuous loop.

Since it's a loop, the interval is still running, even after the content has loaded. We need to remove the interval once the script has finished executing.

```
clearInterval(myInterval)
```

When you test it again, it plays once and stops. The preloader is now working, but there is no visual indicator to notify the viewer at this point.

```
 1  stop();
 2  myInterval = setInterval(preloader,100);
 3  function preloader(){
 4      if(getBytesLoaded()>= getBytesTotal()){
 5          play();
 6          clearInterval(myInterval)
 7      }
 8          myText.text=Math.round(getBytesLoaded()/getBytesTotal()*100)+"%";
 9
10  }
```

Script Assist

T I P

Simulate Download.
PressCtrl+Enter (Windows) or Cmd+Return (Mac OS) twice. Flash simulates an Internet connection, so you get an accurate feel for how long it will take to download the movie; it will also give you time to see the preloaders. You can also find this option by choosing View > Simulate Download.

T I P

Recycle This Script! If you're creating another movie and want to use the same preloader, you don't have to re-create this every time. Just paste this script and the layers onto the first frame of any movie.

74%

---

6. Script Text to Show Progress

So far, so good. Let's build on what we've done to add the text counter. The code is shown on the left. Let's walk through it.

Remember that the text box instance name is "myText." We already had Flash check to see how many bytes have loaded and how many bytes are in the total content. We'll use that same data for the text. In fact, we'll do a little math this time. We want to express the amount loaded as a percentage of total content, so we'll divide the bytes loaded by the total bytes and then multiply it by 100.

```
myText.text=(getBytesLoaded()/get-
BytesTotal()*100);
```

Because we don't want numbers like 24.33345, we'll instruct Flash to round to the nearest whole number.

So we will use the Math.round method

```
myText.text=Math.round
(getBytesLoaded()/
getBytesTotal()*100);
```

We will now have whole numbers counting down. We want to tell the user that the numbers are percentages, so we will need to add a text string to the end, to diplay the percentage sign. The + operator will be used to add the string to what is being displayed.

```
myText.text=Math.
round(getBytesLoaded()/
getBytesTotal()*100)+"%";
```

Test the script again by pressing Ctrl+Enter (Windows) or Cmd+Return (Mac OS). If the content appears too quickly for you to see the text counter, choose View > Simulate Download, and then Control > Play.

```
stop();
myInterval = setInterval(preloader,100);
function preloader(){
    if(getBytesLoaded()>= getBytesTotal()){
        play();
        clearInterval(myInterval)
    }
        myText.text=Math.round(getBytesLoaded()/getBytesTotal()*100)+"%";
        logo.mask._yscale = (getBytesLoaded()/getBytesTotal()*100);
}
```

45%

72%

7. Animate the Mask

The preloader is working, and the text shows progress. But this will be a lot more interesting with some animation. It's time to script the mask, so that the outline fills as the content is loaded.

Start a new line:

```
logo.mask._yscale
```

We want to animate the mask instance, which is inside the logo instance. Use dots rather than slashes to navigate in ActionScipt; this is called dot syntax.

We want to affect the height of the mask, and dynamically scale it using script. If you remember back to your math days, x = horizontal and y = vertical. The mask should change height (_y) in relationship to the percentage of the movie that has loaded. We will use the _yscale property. We will then add our same math that we used before to calculate the percentage.

```
logo.mask._yscale =
(getBytesLoaded()/
getBytesTotal()*100);
```

Although the text and animation lines of script appear after the clear interval command, they are still controlled by the interval. ActionScript doesn't read from the top to the bottom like we do. All our preloader tasks are contained within the same function.

```
1 function onEnterFrame () {
2 attachMovie ("pointer","pointer",100);
3 pointer._x=_xmouse;
4 pointer._y=_ymouse;
5 Mouse.hide()
6 }
```

Custom Mouse Cursor

Replace the standard arrow in your movie with a custom shape, an imported bitmap, or just about anything else you can dream up.

Convert to Symbol dialog

Name: pointer

Type: ○ Movie clip   **Registration:**
○ Button
○ Graphic

Linkage
Identifier: pointer
AS 2.0 class:
Linkage: ☑ Export for ActionScript
☐ Export for runtime sharing
☑ Export in first frame
☐ Import for runtime sharing
URL:

Source
Browse...   **File:**
Symbol...   Symbol name: Symbol 1
☐ Always update before publishing

☐ Enable guides for 9-slice scaling

[OK] [Cancel] [Basic]

1. Prepare the Cursor Symbol

Perhaps the hardest part in creating a custom cursor is deciding what you want to use. We'll create a simple ball as our custom cursor. Select the Oval tool with a red-to-black gradient, and then press the Shift key and drag to draw a circle. Select the circle and press F8 to create a symbol. Name the symbol "pointer," select Movie Clip, set the registration point to the center, and click Advanced to see additional options. Select Export for ActionScript. The identifier, which enables us to target the symbol with ActionScript, is the same as the symbol name by default. Click OK, and Flash adds the movie clip to the library. Delete the symbol from the stage. We'll attach it using ActionScript.

2. Create ActionScript

Open the Actions panel. We'll write a simple script that will tell Flash to attach the movie clip when Flash runs, and to position the movie clip where the mouse is.

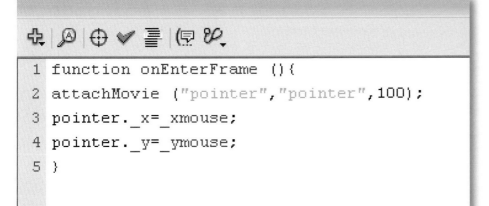

```
1  function onEnterFrame (){
2  attachMovie ("pointer","pointer",100);
3  pointer._x=_xmouse;
4  pointer._y=_ymouse;
5  }
```

To start, we need to use the onEnter-Frame event. That's what tells Flash to perform the function whenever it enters a frame. We want it to load the movie clip from the library and place it on the stage. So we'll use the attachMovie function. We need to provide an ID name, which identifies the movie we're attaching from the library (the identifier we set up in the linkage); a new name, which labels the instance we've created; and depth, which specifies where the symbol should be in the stacking order.

In this case, we're attaching the movie named "pointer," and we can call the instance "pointer," too. We'll use a z depth of 100 so the cursor will always be over other objects.

Now we want to tell Flash where to put the cursor on the stage. It should travel with the mouse. So we always want the pointer's horizontal, or x, position to equal the mouse's x position, and we want their vertical, or y, positions to match as well.

`_xmouse and _ymouse`

To test the script so far, press Ctrl+Enter (Windows) or Cmd+Return (Mac OS). As you move the cursor, the red circle moves with it.

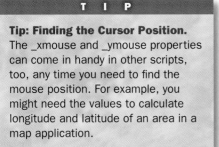

```
function onEnterFrame (){
attachMovie ("pointer","pointer",100);
pointer._x=_xmouse;
pointer._y=_ymouse;
Mouse.hide()
}
```

3. Hide the Default Cursor
Usually, you want to replace the default cursor with your own, so we'll need to hide that arrow. To do so, we'll just add a handy line to the script.:

`Mouse.hide();`

Test the cursor again, and this time, all you see is the custom cursor moving around the screen. Now that you know the basic process, get creative with your cursors! ▥

COLIN SMITH

Click and Drag

Let website visitors be a part of the action by providing a movie clip they can drag around. We'll go one step further in this lesson, making that movie clip a spotlight.

1. Set Up the Images

I'm using the Drag_start.fla file from the How to Wow CD. It's already got an Image layer. Add three more: Actions, Mask, and Dim Image. Then, select the Image layer, and drag the NYC image from the library to the stage.

The image should fill the stage, and it should be perfectly aligned with the top-left corner. To make sure it's aligned, opened the Properties Inspector, and set both the x and y values to 0 **A**.

We'll be using two versions of this image: the original and a dim version. So we need to copy this. Press Ctrl+C (Windows) or Command+C (Mac OS) to copy the image. Then select the Dim Image layer, and choose Edit > Paste in Place. Now there are two copies of the image on two different layers. Hide the Image layer, and then lock both the Image and Dim Image layers.

Soften Fill Edges

Distance: 14 px

Number of steps: 6

Direction: ◉ Expand ○ Inset

OK / Cancel

Properties | Filters | Parameters

Movie Clip

mask

Instance of: mask

Swap...

Color: None

W: 102.8 X: 82.1

H: 102.8 Y: 87.1

Blend: Normal

☑ Use runtime bitmap caching

2. Create the Mask

Select the Mask layer, which is where we want to create the movie clip that will serve as a spotlight. Select the Oval tool, make sure there's no stroke, and set the fill for any color. I'll use dark gray, but it really doesn't matter what color you use. Make sure the Object Drawing button is deselected. Then, hold down the Shift key as you draw a circle.

For a spotlight effect, we'll soften the circle's edges. Select it and choose Modify > Shape > Soften Fill Edges. In the Soften Fill Edges dialog box, set the distance at 14 pixels, the number of steps to 6, and select Expand. Click OK and then deselect the circle to see the effect.

Now, we'll convert the circle to a symbol. Use the Selection tool to drag a marquee around the circle. Then press F8 to convert it to a movie clip symbol. Set the registration to the top left and name the symbol "mask."

We want to control this mask with ActionScript, so we'll need to name the instance. While it's still selected, open the Properties Inspector and type "mask" for the instance name. Select Use Runtime Bitmap Caching as well so that the softened edges work properly.

```
1  mask.onPress = function(){
2      this.startDrag();
3  }
4
```

drag-start.swf

File   View   Control   Debug

NEW YORK CITY

```
1  mask.onPress = function(){
2      this.startDrag();
3  }
4  mask.onRelease = function(){
5      this.stopDrag();
6  }
```

3. Create ActionScript for Dragging the Movie Clip

We're ready to write some ActionScript to let viewers drag this mask around. Select the Actions layer, and then open the Actions panel. We want our script to trigger dragging when the viewer clicks on the mask instance. We'll use the onPress event and the startDrag function. Because the function has already been assigned to the mask instance, we can use the word "this" to refer to it in the script:

```
mask.onPress = function(){
    this.startDrag();
}
```

Test the script by pressing Ctrl+Enter (Windows) or Cmd+Return (Mac OS). Sure enough, when you click the circle, you can drag it. But when you release the mouse, it continues dragging. Let's add some more script to stop it.

Copy the script we've written so far and paste it. You will find that you do a lot of cutting and pasting with code; it saves time. Then replace onPress with onRelease and startDrag with stopDrag.

Test the script again. Now it moves when you drag the mouse, and it stops when you release the mouse. You can use this script to enable dragging for any symbol, whether it's a mask or not. The dragging effect is much easier to achieve than you probably imagined.

T I P

Soft Edges on Masks. In order for a soft-edged mask to display correctly, you must enable Runtime Bitmap Caching on both the mask and the object that you want to mask.

```
mask.onPress = function(){
    this.startDrag();
}

mask.onRelease = function(){
    this.stopDrag();
}

img.setMask(mask);
```

4. Set Up the Mask

Right now, it's just a soft-edged gray circle moving around on top of the photograph. Let's add the spotlight effect. First, we need to darken the image on the Dim Image layer, and then we'll use the mask to reveal the lighter image.

Hide the Image layer, and lock all the layers except the Dim Image layer. To darken the image, we need to convert it to a movie clip symbol. Press F8, and name it "image." In the Properties Inspector, choose Brightness from the Color menu. Lower the brightness to about −70% to make the image quite dark.

Unlock the Image layer, because it's the layer we need to mask. Move the Image layer above the Dim Image layer, so that the bright image appears on top. Select the bright image and press F8 to convert it to a movie clip named imagebright. In the Properties Inspector, name the instance "img," and select Use Runtime Bitmap Caching.

Select the Actions layer, and open the Actions panel. We'll add the line of script that will set the mask. We need to target the "img" instance, using the setMask method and identifying the mask instance.

`img.setMask(mask)`

Test it again. Now you can shift the spotlight from one area of the image to another. ▦

COLIN SMITH

COLIN SMITH

Create a Dynamic Image Gallery

Use the thumbnails you created in Chapter 2 as buttons for an image gallery.

Properties   Filters   Para

Movie Clip

Button 1

1. Prepare Items for Scripts

If you created thumbnails in Chapter 2, open that file again now and we'll create an image gallery to display each of those images full-size. Or, you can open imagegallery-before.fla from the How to Wow CD to find the thumbnails ready to go. We're going to attach a script to each of these thumbnails so that when you click a thumbnail, a full-size version of the image appears. Before we can attach the script, we need to name each of the thumbnails, convert the images to symbols, and link the symbols to ActionScript.

Each thumbnail is an instance of a symbol. We need to name each of the instances so we can identify them in our script. So let's name them btn1, btn2, btn3, and btn4. To name an instance, select it, and then type the name in the Properties Inspector.

To convert an image to a symbol, drag it from the library onto the stage, and then press F8. In the Convert to Symbol dialog box, select the movie clip type and name the symbol. We'll add mc to

each image name to indicate that it's a movie clip: michael_mc, angela_mc, kaysar_mc, and kuntal_mc. Make sure that the registration is set to the top left so that when we provide instructions for positioning, they relate to the upper-left corner. Click OK.

The symbol appears in the library. Delete the image. Do the same to create symbols from the other images.

2. Link Symbols to ActionScript

In order to use these symbols in an ActionScript, we need to export them for ActionScript. Right-click one of the symbols (such as angela_mc) in the library, and choose Linkage (or choose the linkage button in the Library panel). In the Linkage Properties dialog box, select Export for Action Script **A**; the Identifier should have the same name as the movie clip **B**. Click OK, and then create the linkage for each of the other symbols.

3. Create the Initial ActionScript

We're ready to create the script that will open the full-size image when you click its thumbnail. It's always a good idea to create a new layer, named Script, and drag it to the top of the Layers palette.

Select the first frame in the timeline. Then, open the Actions panel at the bottom of the screen. It should be titled Actions-Frame **A**. (If it says Actions-Button, a button is selected. Deselect it and select the first frame in the timeline instead.)

Type this script to open a full-size version of the image of Michael when you click on the thumbnail of Michael:

```
1  btn1.onRelease = function(){
2      attachMovie ("michael_mc","michael",0);
3      michael._x=20;
4      michael._y=120;
5  };
```

```
btn1.onRelease = function(){
attachMovie("michael_mc",
"michael",0);
};
```

When we release the mouse over the thumbnail of Michael, Flash will import the movie clip from the library, name the instance, and place it at a depth of zero.

We need to tell Flash where to position the new image instance:

```
michael._x=20;
michael._y=120;
};
```

Now its upper-left corner (based on the registration point we set earlier) is 20 pixels from the left and 120 pixels from the top of the stage.

4. Test the Script

First, make sure the syntax is valid. Flash can check to see that you've closed brackets and included the information required for your actions. Click the check mark at the top of the Actions panel to check for errors.

To test the script, press Ctrl+Enter (Windows) or Cmd+Enter (Mac OS). Click the first thumbnail. The full image should appear below it.

```
btn1.onRelease = function(){
    attachMovie ("michael_mc","michael",0);
    michael._x=20;
    michael._y=120;
};
btn2.onRelease = function(){
    attachMovie ("angela_mc","angela",0);
    angela._x=20;
    angela._y=120;
};
btn3.onRelease = function(){
    attachMovie ("kuntal_mc","kuntal",0);
    kuntal._x=20;
    kuntal._y=120;
};
```

5. Duplicate and Modify the Script for Other Thumbnails

When you've tested the script for the first thumbnail, all you need to do is copy it and modify it for the others. Select the entire script in the Actions panel and press Ctrl+C (Windows) or Cmd+C (Mac OS) to copy it. Then, press Enter to move down in the screen, and paste the script. Duplicate the script one time for each thumbnail.

Now, change the references in each script for the appropriate thumbnail. Change Btn1 to Btn2, Btn3, or Btn4. Change michael_mc to angela_mc, kaysar_mc, and kuntal_mc. And change michael to angela, kaysar, and kuntal.

To test the full script, press Ctrl+Enter (Windows) or Cmd+Enter (Mac OS), and then click each thumbnail to view the full image.

For best results, try to make your photos the same size and orientation. You can take this further and create a more elegant gallery than what we have here by decorating the background and creating nice frames. ▦

TIP

Shortcut for Instances. For a simple script like this one, you can cheat a little bit, and leave the instance names the same. All you really need to change is the button name and the ID Name (Michael_mc). However, in a more complex script, where instances may be referred to multiple times, it's safer to give each instance a unique name.

INSIGHT

Camel Case. We can't use spaces to separate words in scripts, so most scripters use camel case to make the scripts easier to read. Camel case is the practice of capitalizing each word within a compound word. The name comes from the uppercase "bumps" in the middle of the word, which remind some people of a camel's humps. You may also hear camel case referred to as BiCapitalization, InterCaps, or Mixed Case.

7

NAVIGATING WITH STYLE

Don't settle for boring navigation—lead your visitors with style and let them have some fun.

INVISIBLE BUTTONS *158*

ACTIONSCRIPT *159*

TIMELINE-BASED NAVIGATION *160*

SHELL-BASED NAVIGATION *164*

FOCUS FOR EFFECT *167*

TABBED SLIDER *170*

DROP-DOWN MENUS *175*

NAVIGATION TOOLS HELP your viewers find their way around the website to access content. You can provide simple navigation, with buttons or text links. But with Flash, you can let your creativity fly and design fun and intriguing navigation systems. There are countless examples of innovative navigation on the web. Some of my personal favorites are on the sites for movies and recording artists. As you build your skills in Flash, keep an eye out for sites that delight you.

The most important aspect of navigation is that it work. That is, your viewers need to be able to find their way around. Usability guru Jakob Nielson coined the phrase "mystery meat navigation" for systems that give no clue about the destination you'll reach when you click a button, or how to get where you're trying to go. Make the navigation as visually complex as you like, but keep it simple to use. Viewers want to be able to get to content quickly, so make transitions fast (2–3 seconds max) and clearly label your buttons. Do these things and you'll have a usable site.

In this chapter, you'll create several kinds of useful navigation systems. We'll start with an ActionScript primer, because we're diving into ActionScript

in this chapter. It's unavoidable for navigation. We'll also create invisible buttons, a trick designers use to make any area clickable. Think of invisible buttons as the Flash equivalent of image maps or hot spots.

Many designers find the concept of structuring an entire website in Flash to be mysterious. You're in luck, because I'm going to show you just how easy it is. I'll walk you through two completely different ways to set up an entire site in Flash, and you can use the best method for your project. My goal is to save you the pain of creating the confusing, inefficient sites I have fumbled through in the past. I wish I'd had this book a few years ago!

We'll take a look at a creative way to use photographs for buttons. The flexibility this provides opens up a whole world of possibilities. It's like looking through the lens of a camera and adjusting the focus ring.

Finally, we'll wrap up the chapter with two of the most requested navigation tricks. We'll create a menu that slides

out when you click a tab, and that is hidden when you click the tab again. And of course, we'll create that time-tested favorite, the drop-down menu. Roll the mouse over a button to see a drop-down menu of sublinks. This is a must-have feature for sites that contain several levels of content, or options you want to initially hide.

Use these lessons as springboards for your own projects. Try combining elements from several tutorials to create something unique. Navigation is one of my favorite topics in Flash, and that's a good thing because every site has to have some form of navigation! I hope you enjoy it as well.

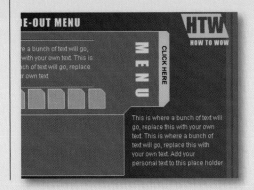

Invisible Buttons

Buttons don't have to have artwork or text, or look like buttons at all. In fact, sometimes it's most effective to use buttons you can't even see.

Why Invisible Buttons?

Suppose you're creating a link from a menu bar, but you don't want the bar to be cluttered with buttons. Often, design decisions preclude the use of traditional buttons. But to script an action, such as going to a frame, playing a movie, or just about anything else, you need something to attach that script to. You need a button.

In fact, the button symbol is useful not only because you can attach script to it, but because it's so easy to make it invisible. Button symbols automatically have four states associated with them, and as long as the Hit state identifies the button area, you don't need to have anything showing for any of the other states. Think of invisible buttons like imageMaps in HTML and JavaScript.

We use invisible buttons in several lessons in this chapter. Keep invisible buttons in mind as you design your own projects. They can give you greater flexibility in designing a site.

Creating Invisible Buttons

Begin creating an invisible button just as you would any other button. Usually, you'll want to create a new layer for the button. Then use one of the drawing tools to draw the button's shape. You can use any fill color; since the button will be invisible, the fill color won't affect the design.

Select the shape you've drawn and press F8 to convert it into a button symbol. Then, double-click the symbol to edit it. As with any button symbol, there are four rollover states in the Timeline. Unlike other button symbols, though, an invisible button only requires the Hit state. So drag the content from the Up state to the Hit state.

Be sure to give the button an instance name in the Properties Inspector. ⌨

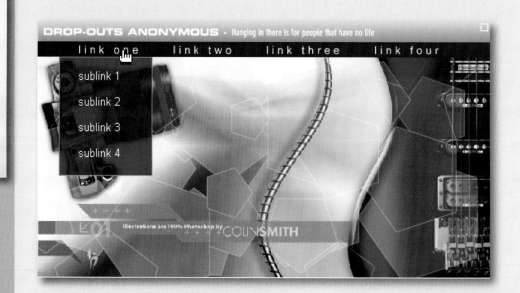

ActionScript Paths and Grammar

In ActionScript it's easy to be confused about the correct syntax to use. We examine the most common use of syntax markup.

Targeting in ActionScript

You can use ActionScript to control the timelines of nested movie clips and even externally loaded movies. If you want to target the main timeline (Scene 1) with ActionScript, use _root from anywhere in any movie.

```
_root.myTimeline.actionsHere
```

If your script is on the main timeline you don't have to write

```
_root
```

To target a nested movie clip, use the instance names to navigate:

```
nav_mc.boxes_mc.actionsHere
```

You are now targeting boxes_mc inside the navigation_mc movie clip. To go back a step, use the keyword _parent. If you're inside boxes_mc and want to talk to the parent clip, navigation_mc, then type

```
_parent.nav_mc.actionsHere
```

To communicate with an externally loaded SWF file, use the instance name of the movie clip that it's loaded into.

Grammar in ActionScript

ActionScript is an event-driven scripting language. Events, such as the click of a button, drive the action. As with any other language, ActionScript has its own vocabulary and grammar. Punctuation is a key part of the scripting grammar.

. A dot serves two purposes. Using dot syntax, you can describe a hierarchy to navigate to a nested movie clip or object. For example, to get to page 42 of this book when it resides on your bookshelf, you would type: bookshelf.howToWow. flash.Page42. You can also use a dot to put a property or a method into a statement. For example, if you're targeting an instance, start the statement with the instance name, followed by a dot.

; A semicolon terminates a statement, which is the equivalent of a sentence.

() Parentheses contain parameters called arguments, which are separated by commas. For example, to play frame 25 of a movie called "myVideo", you'd type

```
gotoAndPlay("myVideo",25);
```

{} Braces contain functions and separate blocks of ActionScript. For example, the function is defined within the braces below:

```
myBtn.onPress = function (){
    gotoAndPlay("movie")
    Mouse.hide();
}
```

COLIN SMITH

Timeline-Based Navigation

Simple timeline techniques make it easier to create an entire website smoothly.

1. Create the Interface

One daunting task in Flash is figuring out how to set up an entire website so that it works and so that you can easily return to edit it. In this lesson, we'll take advantage of the timeline to keep everything tidy and straightforward.

I've opened the Timeline_start.fla file off the How to Wow CD. I've already created an interface for the site in this file. You can create any interface that works for your site. Set that up before you begin fussing with other content. When you do start creating other pages, like the portfolio, contact, home, and info pages here, create each one on its own layer, on a single frame, and then convert it to a symbol. Tour the Timeline_start.fla file to see what I've done here.

We'll mainly be working with the contents of the Home, Portfolio, Info, and Contact layers, scripting buttons to open each of those pages within the interface.

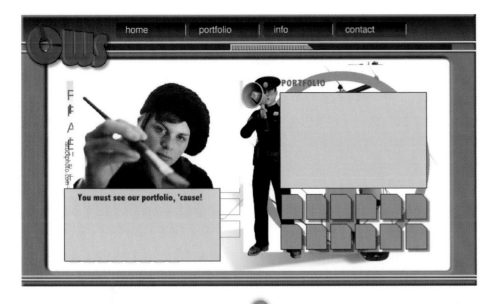

2. Arrange Pages on Different Frames

Currently, all of the content pages are on frame 1, and none of them are visible. We'll need to move them each to their own frame in the timeline.

Start by making all four layers visible, even though it looks like chaos on the stage. Then, we'll create keyframes for each layer in the frame that corresponds with its button position. The keyframe for the Home layer should be in frame 1, and it's already there. So we don't have to do anything with it.

The keyframe for the Portfolio layer should be in frame 2, because the Portfolio button is second. Click frame 1 of the Portfolio layer so that a box appears below the cursor **A**, and then drag the keyframe to frame 2. Now the portfolio page appears on frame 2 **B**.

Drag the keyframe in the Info layer to frame 3, and the keyframe for the Contact layer to frame 4 **C**.

The content pages are on different frames, but the interface is only on frame 1. Of course, we want the interface to appear with all the pages, so we'll need to add layers to it. Open the Interface folder in the timeline, and expand the Timeline window so you can see all the interface layers. Then select frame 4 in the top layer of the interface, press Shift, and select frame 4 in the bottom layer. All the interface layers are selected. Press F5 to create frames 2–4 for each of those layers **D**.

Now the interface appears throughout. To see what we have so far, press Ctrl+ Enter (Windows) or Cmd+Return (Mac OS). The site shows each page in succession, in a continuous loop.

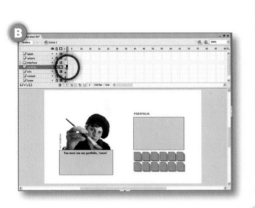

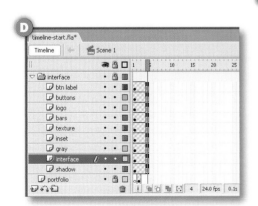

TIP

Red Flags for Labels. When a frame has a label attached to it, Flash displays a small red flag in the frame.

```
1  stop();
```

3. Prepare for Scripting

We want visitors to see the pages they want to see, when they want to see them. So we're going to need to keep Flash from automatically progressing to the next frame, and we'll need to set up the buttons.

First, create a stop action to stop Flash at the first frame. Select the Actions layer, and open the Actions panel. Type

`stop();`

Now, if we test the project, it stops at the home page.

Before we can write any more script, we need to name the button instances we'll be targeting. Select each button, and then type an instance name for it in the Properties Inspector. We'll call them btn1, btn2, btn3, and btn4 **A**.

We also need to be able to tell Flash where to go when the button is pushed. We'll use frame labels to do that. Select the Labels layer. It currently has a keyframe on the first frame, but we need four keyframes. Press F6 three times to add keyframes to frames 2, 3, and 4. Then, select the first frame, and in the Properties Inspector, type home for the frame label. Label frames 2, 3, and 4 portfolio, info, and contact, respectively **B**.

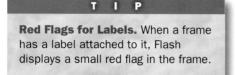

TIP

No Stop Action Required. We don't need to add a stop action to each of the frames, because we're using the gotoAndStop function. Flash is already stopping when it arrives at the frame.

```
stop();

btn1.onRelease = function(){
    gotoAndStop("home");
}
btn2.onRelease = function(){
    gotoAndStop("portfolio");
}
btn3.onRelease = function(){
    gotoAndStop("info");
}
btn4.onRelease = function(){
    gotoAndStop("contact");
}
```

4. Write ActionScript for Buttons

We're ready to script the buttons now. Select the Actions layer and open the Actions panel again.

We want to write a script for the first button (btn1), to take effect as we release the mouse (onRelease), to make Flash go to frame 1 (home) and stop there (gotoAndStop).

```
btn1.onRelease = function(){
    gotoAndStop("home");
}
```

Copy and paste the code three more times, and then substitute the button instance names (btn2, btn3, and btn4) and the frame labels (portfolio, info, and contact) to create scripts for each of the other buttons.

Check for errors, and then press Ctrl+ Enter (Windows) or Cmd+Return (Mac OS) to test the project. It's a fully functional site in a Flash movie. ▦

INSIGHT

Returning Home. Why do we need to create a script to go to the home page, when it appears as soon as the site opens? Because viewers may want to return to the home page after they've visited other pages in your site, and you need to give them a way to get there.

INSIGHT

Pros and Cons. This is a simple, elegant way to build a site. You can see how layers are interacting, edit content easily, and control all the ActionScript from one frame. This method of creating a website works very well if you're working with a simple site that is fairly easy to load. However, if your pages include complex graphics or large movie files, you may prefer to create a shell and load the pages as separate SWF files. I'll show you that option in the next lesson.

Shell-Based Navigation

Create a graphical shell for a website, and then use ActionScript to load external SWF and JPEG files on demand.

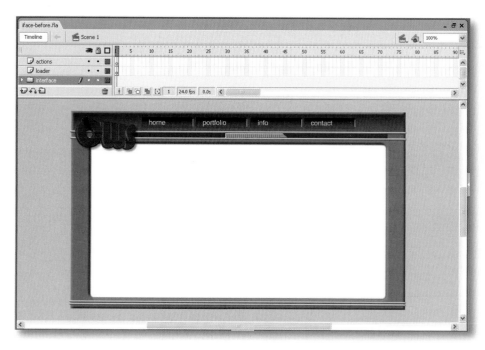

1. Create the Interface for the Shell

We'll use the same interface we used to create timeline-based navigation. However, this time the home, portfolio, info, and contact pages are separate SWF files, rather than layers inside the Flash file. I've opened the iface_before. fla file from the How to Wow CD, and I'll also be using the home.swf, portfolio.swf, info.swf, and contact.swf files off the CD.

The first step to creating shell-based navigation is the same as the first step to creating timeline-based navigation: design the interface and the content. You can tour the layers in this interface to see how I've put it together, but any interface you've designed should work. We'll be creating ActionScript for the buttons to call the external files, so the buttons need instance names. Select each button, and then type a name in the Properties Inspector: btn1, btn2, btn3, and btn4.

If you're working on your own site, create each of the content pages, but instead of placing them on individual layers, export each from Flash as a SWF file. Make sure the content page SWF files are in the same folder as the main SWF file to keep scripting easy.

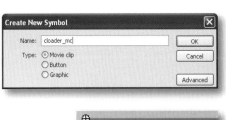

2. Create an Empty Movie Clip

We need to create a new movie clip that will serve as our loader. So let's create one. It doesn't have to have any content. Select the loader layer. Then choose Insert > New Symbol, and make sure its type is Movie Clip. Name it cloader_mc for content loader movie clip. Click OK.

Flash takes us into the clip, so we can add content. But we want to leave this clip empty.

Return to Scene 1. Drag the cloader_mc symbol onto the stage. There's nothing in this symbol, so Flash displays only the registration point. Move the registration point to the upper-left corner of the stage. While it's still selected, name the instance loader_mc in the Properties Inspector.

We'll use this movie clip to load external SWF files, and we want the interface layer to appear above them. So, move the loader layer beneath the Interface layer in the Timeline.

3. Write the ActionScript to Load External Files

We're ready to write some ActionScript. Select the Actions layer, and then open the Actions panel. Here's what we want our script to do: when we click the first button (btn1) and release it (onRelease), we want it to use the loader movie clip

INSIGHT

Loader Movie Clip. As you click a button, Flash loads the appropriate SWF file and it appears quite seamless. No one would guess that the page is not stored in the main file. That's because Flash is treating the external files as if they are part of the Flash file. Flash sees the path to the home page as part of the loader_mc movie clip. Be careful if you're using this technique with external pages that have their own ActionScript included; you may have to include the loader_mc path in their scripts as well.

```
btn1.onRelease = function(){
    loader_mc.loadMovie("home.swf");
}
```

(loader_mc) to load an external movie file (loadMovie) named home.swf.

```
btn1.onRelease = function(){
    loader_mc.loadMovie("home.swf");
}
```

Verify that the syntax is correct. Then press Ctrl+Enter (Windows) or Cmd+Return (Mac OS) to test it. Click the Home button, and the home.swf file loads. That's what we wanted.

Now we need to do the same thing for the other three buttons. Copy and paste the code three times. Then substitute the button names and the file names. Test it again. When you click each button, Flash should load the appropriate SWF file.

TIP

Script Order Doesn't Matter. Flash reads all of the ActionScript at the same time, so it really doesn't matter which order the scripts are in. Organize them in any way that makes the most sense to you, so that you can quickly find the right one to edit it or to troubleshoot a problem.

```
btn1.onRelease = function(){
    loader_mc.loadMovie("home.swf");
}
btn2.onRelease = function(){
    loader_mc.loadMovie("portfolio.swf");
}
btn3.onRelease = function(){
    loader_mc.loadMovie("info.swf");
}
btn4.onRelease = function(){
    loader_mc.loadMovie("contact.swf");
}
onLoad = function(){
    loader_mc.loadMovie("home.swf");
}
```

4. Script the Home Page to Open Immediately

Our buttons are all working, but when you first open the site, the page is blank. The home page should load by default. We can fix that easily enough. Select the Actions layer again and return to the Actions panel. Copy the first script, the one that called the home.swf file, and paste it at the bottom. Remove the reference to btn1, because the home page will appear without anyone pushing any buttons. Then, change onRelease to onLoad. When the page initially loads, Flash will load the home.swf file.

Test the file. As it opens, you see the home page. Click a button to see the corresponding page. This is a great way to build a website! 📖

Focus for Effect

Emphasize selections and make ordinary tasks more fun with rollovers that use blur effects.

COLIN SMITH

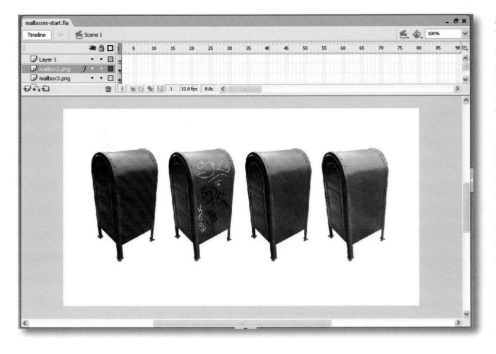

1. Create the Button Images

Why should all buttons be rectangles or ovals? I've opened the Mailboxes_start.fla file off the How to Wow CD. It contains four mailboxes that we can use as buttons. You can use anything as buttons—images of products, images of people, images of traffic signs, whatever you want to use. I took a photograph of a mailbox and then, in Photoshop, cut it out, duplicated it, removed the graffiti using the Healing Brush tool, applied different colors, and saved four separate images. In Flash, I imported the images and placed each on its own layer.

We'll convert these mailboxes to buttons and make them all blurred by default. When the viewer rolls over one with a mouse, it will become clearer and larger, appearing to move forward.

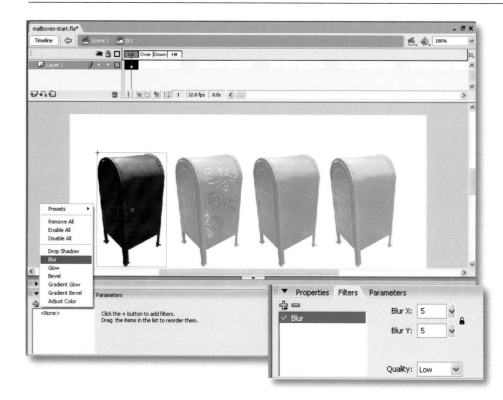

2. Convert the Images to Symbols

First, we'll convert the mailbox images to symbols. Because we want to use the Blur filter, we need to convert them to movie clip symbols. Select the first image and press F8. Select Movie Clip for type and then name it lbr for letter box red. Convert each of the other three mailboxes to movie clips called lbg (for graffiti), lbgr (for gray), and lbgre (for green).

Each mailbox is a movie clip symbol now. But we're not done with them. We need to convert them to buttons so we can quickly and easily apply the roll-over states. Select the first symbol and press F8. Select Button for the type and call it bt1 for button 1.

Convert each of the others to button symbols called bt2, bt3, and bt4.

3. Create the Rollover States

Now, let's use the Blur filter and create the rollover states. Double-click the first button. Because it's a button symbol, we see the rollover states on the timeline. But because there's a movie clip symbol nested inside it, we can apply a filter. Select the Up state in the timeline. Open the Filters panel, click the Plus button, and choose Blur.

Select 5 for the x and y blur values. The Up state is blurred now. Hold down the Alt (Windows) or Option (Mac OS) key as you drag the dot from the Up state into each of the other states.

When the mouse moves over the mailbox, we want it to move into focus. Select the Over state, and then click the symbol again. In the Filters panel, click the Minus sign to remove the blur. We also want to enlarge the mailbox slightly in the Over state. Holding down the

Snapping Limitations. When you want to resize something, the Snap to Objects feature can be a tremendous asset or a frustrating barrier. To resize the mailbox, you may want to turn it off so that you can enlarge the mailbox to exactly the size you want, without worrying about its relationship to the underlying grid or other objects.

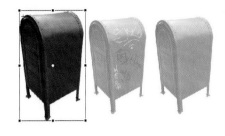

Symbols within Symbols. Though these are movie clip symbols, you can still convert them to button symbols. For each one, Flash nests the movie clip symbol inside the button symbol. This gives us greater flexibility. We can use the quick rollover options in the Button symbol with the filters that are only available to movie clip symbols. Nifty, eh?

Shift key to keep it proportional, use the Free Transform tool to expand the mailbox a little bit.

The first mailbox is all set. Return to Scene 1. Double-click the second mailbox and create the same rollover states for it, and then do the same for the third and the fourth.

To test the buttons in Flash, return to Scene 1, and choose Control > Enable Simple Buttons. Roll over each button to see its behavior.

To test the effect further, press Ctrl+ Enter (Windows) or Cmd+Return (Mac OS) and roll over each mailbox. As you roll over one, it comes into focus, commanding the viewer's full attention and appearing as if it is moving in three-dimensional space. ▥

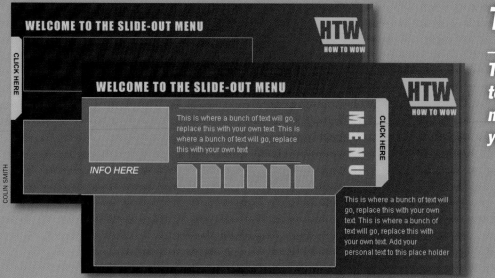

Tabbed Slider

There's no reason for buttons to be static. Create a cool menu that slides out when you click its tab.

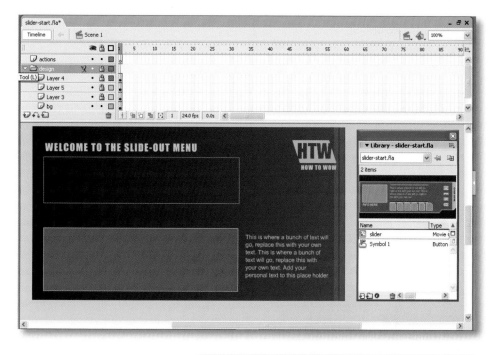

1. Create a Placeholder for the Slider

Sliding menus make a website more interesting—and they can help you save valuable screen real estate when they're closed. I've opened the Slider_start.fla file off the How to Wow CD. The file already includes several layers that make up the basic interface; most of the layers are nested in a folder called Design. I've already created a movie clip for the sliding menu, and it's in the Library.

Create a new layer called Slider. We won't just drag the slider symbol onto the main stage, though. If we did, we'd end up with a complicated set of keyframes in the main timeline. In this case, we're going to use just a single frame in Scene 1 and include all the animations in movie clips.

Instead of dragging the slider symbol onto the stage, we'll create an empty movie clip and nest the slider inside it. With the Slider layer selected, choose Insert > New Symbol. Select Movie Clip for the type and name it placeholder.

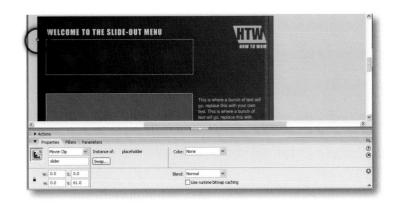

When you click OK, Flash opens the placeholder symbol so you can edit it. It's empty, and we're going to leave it empty, so return to Scene 1. The placeholder symbol has been added to the Library.

Drag the placeholder symbol onto the stage. All that appears is a registration point. Move it up to the left-hand side; select it and give it an instance name of slider.

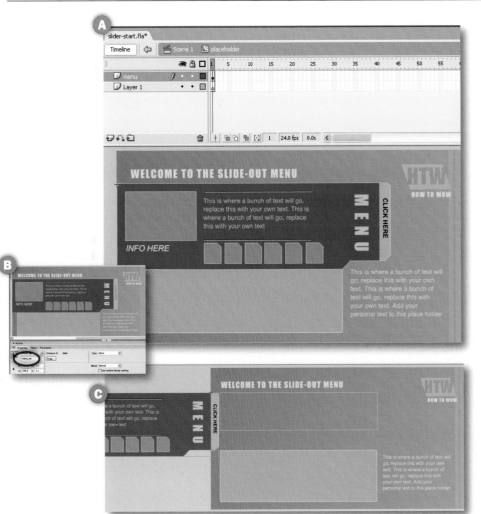

2. Animate the Slider

As its name suggests, the slider needs to move back and forth. We'll edit the placeloader movie clip to animate the slider. Double-click the registration point on the placeholder symbol. Flash opens the movie clip in context, so we can set its position on the stage.

Add a layer named Menu. Then, drag the slider symbol from the Library into its fully extended position **A**.

Select the slider and name the instance menu_mc. We will need an instance name so that we can control it **B**.

Select frame 10 in the Menu layer, and press F6 to create a keyframe. Then, right-click (Windows) or Control-click (Mac OS) between frames 1 and 10, and choose Create Motion Tween. Select frame 1 and drag the slider off the screen, so that only the tab is on the stage **C**. Now when you scrub through the timeline, the slider moves onto the stage.

Next, we need to make the slider move back off the stage. Press Alt (Windows) or Option (Mac OS) and drag the first keyframe to frame 15. Then create another motion tween between frames 10 and 15. It'll take longer for it to slide out than it does to return to the tab.

We'll add stop actions so that the slider doesn't just slide in and out continuously. Drag Layer 1 above the Menu layer, and then select frame 10 and press F6 to create a keyframe. Open the Actions panel and type stop(); to add a stop action. Do the same for frame 1, so that the slider won't automatically open when the page loads. When you click the tab, Flash will move through the timeline until it hits another stop action, and the slider will stay in the open position. When you click the tab again, the slider will close. There's no stop action at the end, so the timeline will loop back to frame 1.

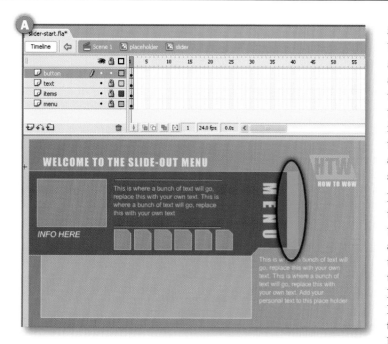

3. Attach a Button to the Slider

We want the slider to open when someone clicks the tab, so we need to attach a button. If we attached it to the tab in the main scene, we'd have to have two: one in the open position and one in the closed position. We'd also have to track the button. It's much easier to attach an invisible button to the slider, so that the button is always with it.

Double-click the slider symbol. Lock all the layers except the Button layer. Use the Rectangle tool with no stroke and any fill color to draw a button over the tab **A**. Select the button and press F8 to convert it to a button symbol named Invs. Double-click the button to edit it. Because the button should be invisible, the only state we need is the Hit state. Drag the frame from the Up state onto the Hit state, which will define its shape and area **B**.

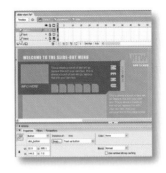

We'll need to refer to this button in ActionScript, so it needs an instance name. Double-click on the slider again to return to the slider movie clip.

Then, select the button and open the Properties Inspector. Type click_button for the instance name.

```
slider.menu_mc.click_button.onRelease = function (){
    slider.play(nextFrame);
}
```

4. Write ActionScript for the Button

With everything named, we're ready to write the ActionScript. We'll use several instances: slider, which is the empty movie clip; menu_mc inside the slider movie clip; and click_button, inside the menu_mc clip. We need to remember how they're nested so that we can write the correct path. To refer to the click_button instance, we'll need to type slider.menu_mc.click_button.

Return to Scene 1. Select the Actions layer and then open the Actions panel.

When we click the button (slider. menu_mc.click_button) and release it (onRelease), we want to play (play) the next frame (nextFrame) in the slider movie clip (slider).

```
slider.menu_mc.click_button.¬
onRelease = function(){
    slider.play(nextFrame);
}
```

Press Ctrl+Enter (Windows) or Cmd+Return (Mac OS) to test the movie. When you click the button, the slider slides out. Click it again, and it slides in.

T I P

Name As You Go. You may want to make a habit of naming instances of movie clips right away, so that you don't have to add names multiple times for different keyframes.

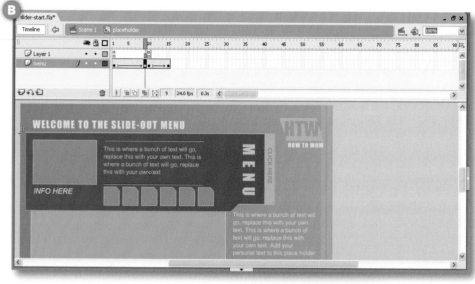

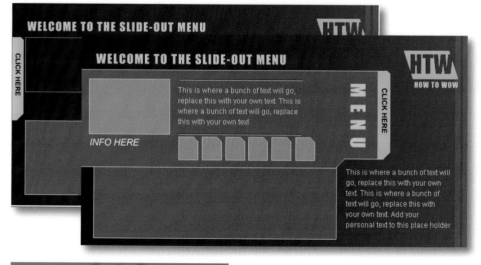

5. Tweak the Slider's Movement

Once the slider's working, you can get more creative with your animation. We'll add some ease to this one, so that it starts fast and slows down as it finishes moving. Double-click the slider to edit the placeholder movie clip. Select the first frame of the Menu layer. Open the Properties Inspector, and set the easing to 100% out **A**. Then select frame 10 and do the same thing.

We'll also add a little springiness to the movement, so that it overshoots the mark a little bit and bounces back to the proper place. Select frame 9 in the Menu layer, and press F6 to create a keyframe **B**. Then nudge the slider a few pixels past its final position. That will give it some spring when it opens. To do the same when it closes, add a keyframe to frame 14 and drag the slider further off the stage by a few pixels. Experiment a bit. Test it and tweak it until it has the effect you want. ▥

T I P

Multiple Menus. You're not limited to one slider. You can attach others to different parts of the page. That's why instance names are such handy identifiers. Without them, clicking one tab would open all the sliders.

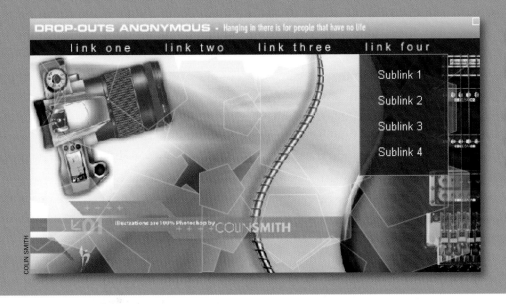

Drop-down Menus

Create drop-down menus in Flash to bring elegance and style to your website.

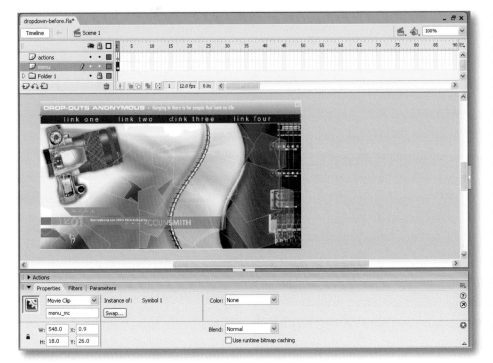

1. Create the Menu Bar

Many websites are several pages deep, and drop-down menus are an efficient, intuitive way to navigate a site. As you roll over the main menu, submenus will appear so that you can click the appropriate link. I'm using the Dropdown_before.fla file from the How to Wow CD.

The menu bar is in the library. I've already positioned it on the interface. You can design any menu bar you want This one is a horizontal menu bar that spans the width of the page. It just a gray rectangle with some text added to it and I converted it to a movie clip. We still need to give it an instance name, though. Select the menu bar and open the Properties Inspector. Name the instance menu_mc for menu movie clip.

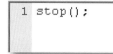

2. Label Frames

Double-click the menu_mc instance to edit it. One layer, Menu, is already there. Create three new layers, naming the top one Labels, the next one Menu Text, and the third one Submenu. Then, move the Submenu layer below the Menus layer **A**.

Because we have four items in the menu bar, we'll need four submenus. We'll use the timeline to script when they should appear. Select the Labels layer, and press F6 to create keyframes at frames 5, 10, 15, and 20. The Menu layer also needs to have 20 frames, so select frame 20 and press F5.

To script the submenus efficiently, we'll label the keyframes in the Labels layer. Select the first keyframe, at frame 1, and label it Start. We'll use that label when there's no submenu showing. Label frames 5, 10, 15, and 20 l1, l2, l3, and l4, respectively **B**. Then, to keep Flash from looping through the submenus, we'll add a stop action to each label. Select the first one, open the Actions panel, and type stop();. Do the same for each of the others.

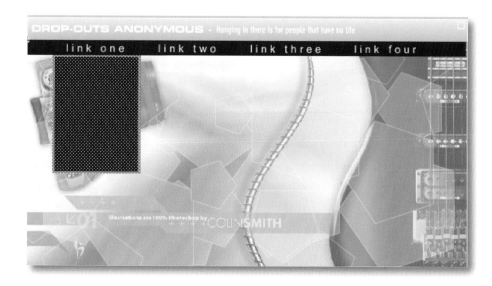

3. Create the Submenu

You can be as fancy as you like when you design the submenus for your site. For this project, though, we'll keep it quite simple. Lock all the layers except the Submenu layer. Select the Rectangle tool, with a bright orange stroke and a dark gray fill. Draw a rectangle under Link One. Double-click it to select both the fill and the stroke and press F8 to convert the rectangle to a movie clip called Sub (for submenu).

We're keeping this simple, but let's dress it up a little bit by adding some transparency. Select the submenu and open the Properties Inspector. Choose Alpha from the Color menu, and drop the opacity to 75%.

T I P

Use _root to Navigate. Because the sublinks are inside another movie clip, use the keyword _root if you are targeting other portions of the same site. This will make the navigation start at the top level, for example _root.movie_mc.gotoAndPlay.

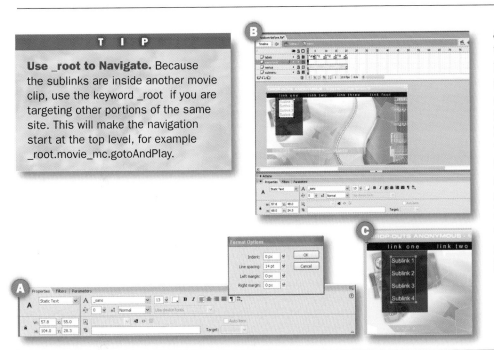

4. Add the Text to the Submenu

We're ready to add text to the submenu. Unlock the Menu Text layer and lock the Submenu layer. Select the first frame of the Menu Text layer. Then, select the Text tool, with a white fill. In the Properties Inspector, set the text size to 13 and choose Static Text **A**. Now, type Sublink 1 in the submenu, and then add text for three more links **B**. For a real-world site, you'd use meaningful link names, of course.

To position the text, move it to the middle of the submenu. Then, in the Properties Inspector, click the paragraph symbol to open the Format Options dialog box. Change the line spacing to provide more space between the links **C**.

5. Create Keyframes for Submenu Locations

Move the Menu Text layer just above the Submenu layer. There's only one frame in the Menu Text layer. Select frame 20 and press F5 to fill in the frames. Do the same with the Submenu layer.

Right now, if you previewed the movie, the submenu would appear immediately, because it's on the first keyframe in the Submenu and Menu Text layers. The submenu shouldn't appear until the menu link is clicked. Unlock all the layers. Then, select the first keyframes in the Menu Text and Submenus layers, and drag them to frame 5. Now the submenu appears on frame 5, but not on frame 1 **A**.

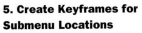

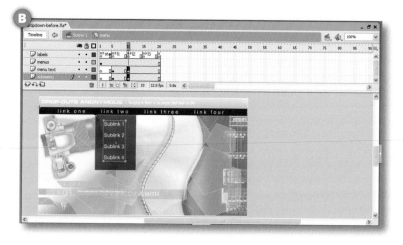

Select the Submenu and menu text keyframes at frame 5 and press Alt (Windows) or Option (Mac OS) as you drag a copy to frame 10. Then, drag the submenu and the menu text below Link 2 on the menu bar **B**. In fact, you can just press the arrow key to nudge the submenu over (holding Shift in addition moves it faster). Copy the keyframe to frames 15 and 20, nudging the submenu to Link 3 and Link 4.

When the timeline starts, there's a stop action, and no submenu appears. When you roll over link one, Flash will display the first submenu (frame 5); when you roll over link two, Flash will display the second submenu (frame 10); and so on.

6. Create Invisible Buttons for Menu Bar

The submenu's in good shape, but we need buttons to attach them to on the menu bar. Return to Scene 1. We'll create invisible buttons. Add a new layer called Buttons, and lock all the other layers. Select the Rectangle tool with no stroke and any color fill. Draw a button that covers the menu item.

Select the button, press F8 to convert it to a button symbol, and name it Invis. Double-click the button to edit it. Because it's a button symbol, there are four rollover states. For an invisible button, we only need the Hit state, which identifies the button area. Drag the keyframe from the Up state to the Hit state.

Return to Scene 1. Select the button, and name its instance btn1. To duplicate the button for the other menu items, press Alt (Windows) or Option (Mac OS) and drag it into position. Name the instances btn2, btn3, and btn 4. Don't worry about

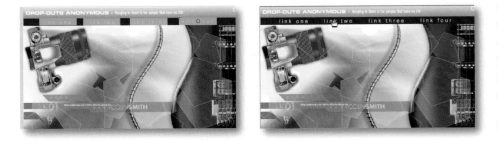

the button color; it will be invisible in the movie. Lock the Buttons layer.

Test the movie so far by pressing Ctrl+Enter (Windows) or Cmd+Return (Mac OS). When you move the mouse over the buttons, Flash changes the cursor to indicate a button, but the button itself is invisible.

```
btn1.onRollOver = function (){
    menu_mc.gotoAndPlay("l1");
}
```

7. Write ActionScript to Display the Submenus

The pieces are in place. Now we just need to write some ActionScript to pull it all together. Select frame 1 in the Actions layer and open the Actions panel.

When we roll the mouse over (onRollOver) the first button (btn1), we want Flash to play (gotoAndPlay) the menu movie clip (menu_mc) at the first keyframe, which we gave a label ("l1"). We'll use a function to do this.

```
btn1.onRollOver = function(){
    menu_mc.gotoAndPlay("l1");
}
```

Verify that the syntax is correct, and then press Ctrl+Enter (Windows) or Cmd+Return (Mac OS) to play the movie. The first submenu appears when you roll over the first menu item.

Copy the script and paste it three more times for the other menu buttons. Substitute btn2 and "l2" for the first copy, btn3 and "l3" for the second, and btn4 and "l4" for the third. Test the movie again. Rolling over each link should make its submenu appear.

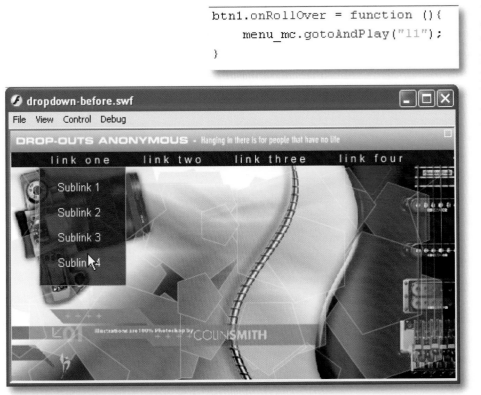

T I P	

Remembering Names. If you've forgotten what you named an instance, select it and open the Properties Inspector. You can do this in the middle of writing the ActionScript, but the process will be smoother if you look up all the names before you start writing the code.

```
btn1.onRollOver = function (){
    menu_mc.gotoAndPlay("l1");
}
btn2.onRollOver = function (){
    menu_mc.gotoAndPlay("l2");
}
btn3.onRollOver = function (){
    menu_mc.gotoAndPlay("l3");
}
btn4.onRollOver = function (){
    menu_mc.gotoAndPlay("l4");
}
```

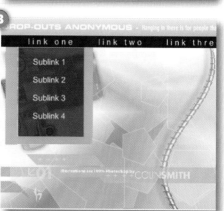

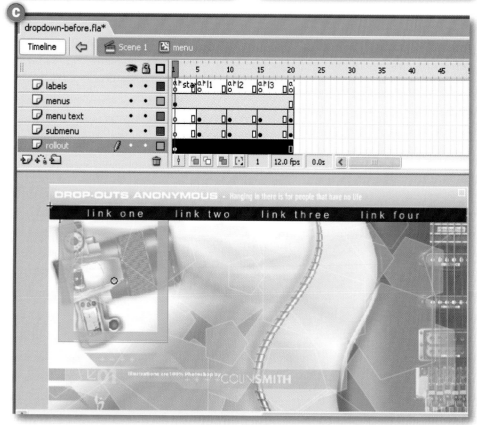

8. Add an Invisible Button to Hide Submenus

The submenus show up when you roll over the main menu items, but once you've uncovered a submenu, there's no way to hide them all. We'll fix that by returning to the menu movie clip. Double-click anywhere on the menu bar to edit it. Create a new layer called Rollout, and drag it to the bottom of the layers in the Timeline **A**.

We'll create a new button that surrounds the submenu. Select frame 5 of the Rollout layer. Select the Rectangle tool with no stroke and any color fill, turn Object Drawing off, and draw three rectangles around the submenu. To prevent confusion, avoid overlapping the button on the menu bar **B**.

Double-click the area you've drawn to select it, and press F8 to convert it to a button symbol called Rollout.

Double-click the button to edit it. Like the menu buttons, we want this one to be invisible. Drag the contents of the Up state to the Hit state.

Then return to the menu symbol. Name the instance rollout_btn **C**.

Of course, we'll need one of these buttons for each of the submenus. Create keyframes at frames 10, 15, and 20, and drag the surrounding button to match the submenu for each of the frames.

We'll need to target this button with ActionScript, so it needs to be present on the first frame, but we don't actually want it on the screen. So copy the rollout button to Frame 1 of the Rollout layer and position the button off the stage **D**. This way we can target our ActionScript without the button appearing on the stage.

```
btn1.onRollOver = function(){
    menu_mc.gotoAndPlay("11");
}
btn2.onRollOver = function(){
    menu_mc.gotoAndPlay("12");
}
btn3.onRollOver = function(){
    menu_mc.gotoAndPlay("13");
}
btn4.onRollOver = function(){
    menu_mc.gotoAndPlay("14");

}


menu_mc.rollout_btn.onRollOver = function(){
    menu_mc.gotoAndStop("start");

}
```

9. Use ActionScript to Hide Submenus

Now we can use ActionScript to target the invisible button we just created. Return to Scene 1. Then select the Actions layer and open the Actions panel.

We want to target the rollout button (rollout_btn), which is inside the menu movie clip (menu_mc), so we'll use dot notation to list that path as

```
menu_mc.rollout_btn.
```

When the mouse rolls over (onRollOver) the rollout button, we want it to go to the first frame (labeled "start") and stop. (gotoAndStop).

```
menu_mc.rollout_btn.onRollOver =¬
function(){
    menu_mc.gotoAndStop("start");
}
```

You don't even have to copy the script multiple times, because all the rollout buttons have the same instance name. Test the movie. When you roll over an item in the menu bar, its submenu opens. When you roll away, its submenu closes. ▥

T I P

Take It Further. I've shown you the basic technique, but you can combine it with other Flash techniques to animate the drop-down menus so that they expand or fade or do just about anything else!

8

ADDING VIDEO AND AUDIO

Involve all the senses by adding video and sound

WORKING WITH FLV VIDEO *184*

CREATING A CUTOUT VIDEO *186*

KEYING GREEN SCREEN *188*

CARTOON VIDEO *190*

OLD-TIME CINEMA EFFECT *192*

SKINNING VIDEO COMPONENTS *195*

CREATING VIDEO SILHOUETTES *196*

ADDING SOUND TO A BUTTON *198*

ADDING BACKGROUND MUSIC TO A WEBSITE *200*

ONE OF THE BIGGEST changes in Flash Professional 8 has been its strong support for video. Video may even have been what sparked your interest in Flash. For starters, Flash now uses the On2 VP6 format, which allows us to use high-quality video with a small file size. The On2 VP6 format for video is suitable for streaming on the Internet or for progressive download from a disc. This format also supports alpha channels, so that you can remove the background from a video and have a person walk out onto your web page.

The green screen technique that used to be the domain of big-budget studios is now available to anyone with a home camcorder and a little ingenuity. We'll spend a little time on the green screen technique in this chapter, discussing its setup, screens, and lighting, so you can capture your own video. Then I'll show you how to key out the green in video-editing software such as Adobe After Effects, so that you are left with a transparent alpha channel. Finally, we'll export the video into a format that works in Flash and merge the subject with a new background. As always, the practice files are on the How to Wow CD, so you can have fun with these

techniques before you even plug in your camcorder.

The Flash Video component, new in Flash 8, makes it easy to add video to your Flash projects. We'll explore a couple different methods for pulling video in.

And if you're a special effects freak, don't worry. Three fun and cool projects were designed with you in mind. First, you'll convert video to look like cartoon animation; it's easy but it will look like you spent hours fussing with it.

Then, we'll make modern video look like an old-time movie, converting it to grayscale and adding a sepia tone. For an authentic look, we'll add lines, hairs, scratches, and some flickering.

If you've spent much time on this planet lately, you've certainly seen an Apple iPod commercial, with the dancing silhouettes. Inspired by those commercials, I'll show you how to create your own dancing silhouettes in Flash.

But, wait! There's more. We delve into the realm of sound in this chapter, too, adding clicking sounds to buttons and looping background music to your websites. Video and audio in Flash—let the fun begin!

Working with FLV Video

Export Flash Video files from video-editing applications for use in your Flash projects.

T I P

Converting Video to FLV Format.
You don't have to export a video file in FLV format. You can convert one or more files separately before importing them into Flash using the Flash 8 Video Encoder that comes with Flash Professional 8.

About Using Video in Flash

Flash Video Encoding Settings

Please select a Flash Video encoding profile:

Custom

Custom Settings

Hide Advanced Settings

00:00:00.000

Encoding

☑ Encode video

Video codec: On2 VP6   Quality: Medium

☑ Encode alpha channel   Max data rate: 400   Kilobits per second

Frame rate: Same as source fps   ☐ Resize video

Width:

Key frame placement: Automatic   Height: pixels

Key frame interval: frames   ☐ Maintain aspect ratio

☐ Encode audio

Audio codec: MPEG Layer III (MP3)   Data rate: 96 kbps (stereo)

OK   Cancel

Recent versions of Flash have included strong support for video files, and designers are taking advantage of that. Flash supports its native format, Flash Video, or FLV files. You can export FLV files from several popular video-editing applications, or convert existing files into FLV files using the Flash 8 Video Encoder application that is included with Flash 8 Professional.

You can use the new FLVPlayback component or ActionScript to control video playback and give your users control as they interact with the video. You can use Flash Communication Server or FVSS to stream video, but if you don't have access

to those services, you can use progressive downloading to publish video files that will start playing while the video is downloading.

You can import video clips in FLV format directly into the Flash Library, using encoding options already applied to the files. If you want to make changes frame-by-frame, you can import a video as a frame sequence.

Once you have a video file in Flash, you can convert it to a movie clip symbol and apply interesting effects to it, just as you can to other movie clip symbols.

Exporting to FLV from a Video-Editing Application

Flash Video Encoding Settings

Please select a Flash Video encoding profile:

Flash 8 – Medium Quality (400kbps)

Video encoded for playback with Flash Player 8
Video codec: On2 VP6
Video data rate: 400kbps
Audio codec: MPEG Layer III (MP3)
Audio data rate: 96kbps (stereo)

00:00:00.000

Hide Advanced Settings

Encoding | Cue Points | Crop and Trim

☑ Encode video

Video codec: On2 VP6

☐ Encode alpha channel

Frame rate: Same as Source fps

Key frame placement: Automatic

Key frame interval: _____ frames

Quality: Medium

Max data rate: 400 kilobits per second

☐ Resize video

Width: _____
Height: _____   pixels

☑ Maintain aspect ratio

☐ Encode audio

Audio codec: MPEG Layer III (MP3)

Data rate: 96 kbps (stereo)

Cancel   OK

When you install Flash Professional 8 and QuickTime 6.1.1, the FLV QuickTime Export plug-in is automatically installed to export FLV files from several video-editing applications, including Adobe After Effects, Apple QuickTime Pro, Sorenson Squeeze and Avid Xpress DV. Using this plug-in, you can specify encoding options as you export the file, so that they're ready to use when you import them into Flash.

How you access the plug-in is different in each application. Refer to the application's manual or help files to see how to export an FLV file.

There are several settings you can select for exported video. For most purposes, use the On2 VP6 codec, which supports the alpha channel and keeps file sizes small. If you've keyed something out from a green screen, select Encode Alpha Channel.

You can raise or lower the frame rate, depending on how you'll publish the file. If you're going to publish over the web, you might want to lower the frame rate to 10 or fewer frames per second. Typically, though, video is broadcast at 29.97 frames per second using the NTSC

standard, so 30 fps is pretty close. For Key Frame Placement, choose Automatic.

The quality options change how large the file will be. If you choose Low, the video will use 150 kilobits per second (kb/s). Medium uses 400; and High uses 700. There's no good formula for choosing the quality or for selecting a custom setting. The best option depends on the particular video—how much objects move in the video, how much contrast there is between foreground and background colors, whether the video includes screen capture—and whether you're planning to deliver the movie over the web, a CD, or broadcast media. Experiment with the settings to see which gives you the best quality without increasing the file size more than necessary.

Usually, you'll want to keep the aspect ratio the same. However, you can choose a different aspect ratio, measured in pixels or percentages.

For audio settings, use Mono if you're distributing the video over the web, and 32kb/s produces good sound quality with a small file size. However, if you're producing a CD-ROM, use Stereo, and choose 96 or 128kb/s, depending on how much space you have. ▨

COLIN SMITH

Creating a Cutout Video

Put a subject in front of a matte using imported video with a keyed-out green screen.

1. Prepare the Video File

As long as people have been shooting video, they have been merging different shots to create new stories, and you can do it, too. First, shoot the video of your subject in front of a green screen, and key out the green screen in a video-editing application such as Adobe After Effects or Apple Final Cut Pro. Then export the video in FLV format with Encode Alpha Channel selected.

2. Import the Video into Flash

Open the Flash document you want to use the video file in. I'm using the Greenscreen_before.fla file from the How to Wow CD. A background is already in place. Choose Import > Import Video. In the Import Video dialog box, click Browse and navigate to the FLV file you want to import. For my project, I'll import the Dance short.flv file. Click Next. In the next screen, select Progressive Download from a Web Server, and click Next.

In the Skinning section, choose None, so that no video controls appear on screen. Click Next, and then click Finish.

3. Position the Video

Flash imports the video onto the stage. It doesn't look like much. You can see the boundaries of the video, with a video icon in the center. Postion the box where you want the video to play. To preview the final file, press Ctrl+Enter (Windows) or Cmd+Return (Mac OS). Christie, our dancer, appears in the road, with her original background transparent. █

greenscreen-before.swf

File   View   Control   Debug

Keying Green Screen

To prepare video for your Flash project, remove the green background in a video production application.

Shooting Green Screen

COLIN SMITH

For decades, film professionals have been shooting subjects in front of blue or green screens, removing, or keying, the blue or green background, and compositing their subjects on other backgrounds. Blue screens are the best choice for traditional compositing, but green screens provide better results for digital video.

For the best results, you can rent green fabric that is specifically designed for filming. However, you can create your own green background using any materials, even paint. In my case I have used a muslin sheet on a frame. I have used five lights to get the correct lighting for the green screen projects in this book. You can see the picture of the setup in my garage.

Shooting in front of a green screen takes practice. It's important to light the space evenly, with backlighting for the subject, as well as lighting behind the camera. Allow extra time when you're getting used to the technique, and practice with a patient model.

Lighting Setup

When lighting a green screen, you will need to set up two lights for the screen and try to light it evenly. Try diffusing the light with softboxes or reflectors.

Set up a back light that hits the rear of the subject; this will provide seperation from the background.

Place your key light off to the side and front; this is your main light for the subject. Use another light or reflector for the fill light, to fill in shadows on the opposite side of the subject.

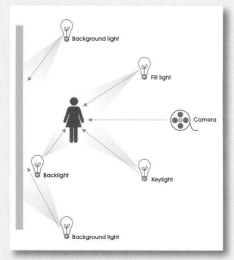

Removing the Green Background

The goal is to capture the subject without any background. We shoot against a green screen because it's easier to remove a consistent, solid background color. You can remove the green background using After Effects, Final Cut Pro, Commotion Pro, Motion, Premiere, or other video production software such as the Keylight Plug-in. I have used After Effects here. The principles are the same for most video applications.

Import the video into your video production application, and drag it to the Timeline. Make any adjustments to its size or rotation that you need to make. For example, this video was shot at 90 degrees and rotated in a video-editing application, leaving black bars on the sides; I changed the size of the composition to remove the bars.

To key the green background, use filters. The specific filters will have different names in different applications, but their functions will be similar. In After Effects, use the Color Range filter to remove the bulk of the green background. (Choose Effect > Keying > Color Range to apply it.) Use the Eyedropper tool to select the green background, and then increase the Fuzziness setting to remove more of it. To clean up the rest of the green, use the Matte Choker and Spill Suppressor effects. (Choose Effect > Matte > Matte Choker and Effect > Keying > Spill Suppressor.)

You'll probably have to tweak several settings to remove most of the green background without compromising the edges of your subject. If you shoot high-definition video on a high-definition camera, you will get a cleaner background.

Exporting Video for Flash

When you've keyed the background so that it is transparent, export the video for use in Flash. In After Effects, choose File > Export > Flash Video (FLV). In other applications, you may need to choose to export to QuickTime to see the Flash export options.

In the Flash Video Encoding Settings dialog box, click Advanced. Select Encode Alpha Channel. This option is critical. If it's not selected, the background won't be transparent when you import the video into Flash.

If you're not using audio, deselect Encode Audio to reduce the file size. You can adjust other settings, such as quality, to meet the needs of your project and the method you'll use to distribute it. Click OK, and name the file.

In Flash, you can either create the FLVPlayback component and use the contentPath field to import the video, or you can choose File > Import > Import Video.

COLIN SMITH

Cartoon Video

Transform real-life video with a cartoon or hand-painted effect.

1. Prepare the Flash Document

First, create a new Flash document with a stage size of 720 x 480 pixels and a frame rate of 16 fps. Then, create a new movie clip to contain the video. Choose Insert > New Symbol, select Movie Clip for the Type, and name it Video. We'll put all the frames into a single clip so that we can easily position the whole video on the stage. You may have to change the frame rate later to get the right speed. For this project, 16 fps looked just about right.

2. Import the Frames as a Sequence

The key to giving standard video a hand-painted look is to import the frames as an image sequence. With the Video movie clip open, choose File > Import > Import to Stage. Navigate to the Dancing clips folder from the How to Wow CD. There are 105 files, each a separate frame from the video. Select the first file and click Open. Because all 105 files have the same file name,

Flash prompts you to import them as a sequence. Click Yes.

Flash imports all the files, adding a keyframe for each file. Return to Scene 1. The clip doesn't appear. Drag the Video movie clip symbol from the library onto the stage and position it so that its upper-left corner matches the stage's upper-left corner. Type 0 for the x and y coordinates in the Properties Inspector.

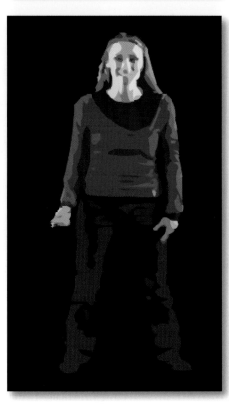

3. Convert Each Frame to a Bitmap

Now we just need to convert each frame to a bitmap. Double-click the video to open the Video symbol. Select the first keyframe. Then select the PNG image on the stage, and choose Modify > Bitmap > Trace Bitmap. Set the Threshold to 100, and Minimum Area to 8. The image changes, so that it looks hand-drawn. Apply the Trace Bitmap command to the image in each keyframe.

It's tedious to change settings in the Trace Bitmap dialog box for each keyframe. Team up the History panel with a custom command to make things go more quickly. Choose Window > Other Panels > History to open the History panel. Then, select the Trace Bitmap command and choose Save As Command. Name the command Trace Bitmap, and click OK. Now, you can apply the exact settings simply by selecting the image and choosing Commands > Trace Bitmap. To make your life even easier, create a keyboard shortcut for the new command: choose Edit > Keyboard Shortcuts, and assign the shortcut. ▥

COLIN SMITH

Creating an Old-Time Cinema Effect

No one needs to know that you shot the video yesterday. Use these techniques to age your movie almost instantly.

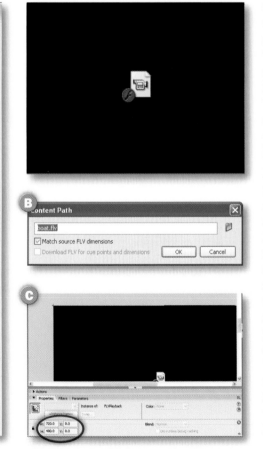

1. Import the Video

Create the video file in a video-editing application, and export it as an FLV file. Then, in Flash, open the Components panel and the Components Inspector. (Choose Window > Components and Window > Components Inspector to open them.) To work along with me, open the Oldfilm_start.fla file from the How to Wow CD.

Drag the FLVPlayback component from the Components panel onto the stage. We'll import the video into this component. Now, in the Components Inspector, select the Parameters tab. Click in the Value column of the ContentPath field, and then click the magnifying glass in that column **A**. In the Content Path dialog box, click the file folder and then navigate to the video you want to import **B**. For this project, select the Boat.flv file from the How to Wow CD, and click OK. The Boat.flv file is the same size as the stage. To position it to fit the stage exactly, select it, and type 0 for the x and y coordinates in the Properties Inspector **C**.

We can't see what's in our video on the stage. To see what you've imported, press Ctrl+Enter (Windows) or Cmd+ Return (Mac OS). I already put a few scratches and lines in, to save time later, but the movie is still in color.

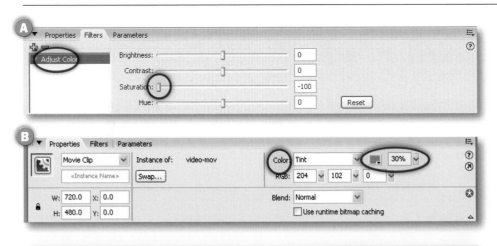

2. Replace the Color with a Sepia Tone

The current video is color. When you select the component, there aren't many options in the Properties Inspector, the Filters panel, or the Parameters panel. We want to apply a filter to this video, and to do that, we need to convert it to a movie clip symbol. Select the video and press F8. Select Movie Clip for the symbol type, and name it video-mov.

Now, open the Filters panel, click the Plus icon, and choose Adjust Color. Move the Saturation slider all the way to the left **A**. Test the results; the movie is black and white now.

To age to this movie, we want to add a sepia tone, which is a yellow-brown tint. So, select the movie clip instance and open the Properties Inspector. Choose Tint from the Color menu. Select a rusty brown color, and then change the tint to 30% **B**. You may need to try a few different colors to find just the right one, but this gives a decent old-time effect. Test it to see how it looks.

3. Add Scratches

Old films have a lot of scratches from dust, hair, and other particles on the film itself or in the projector. I've already created several scratches on the Oldfilm_start.fla file, but we'll add a few more. Choose the Scratches layer and

unlock it. I've created a movie clip to contain the scratches. Double-click a scratch to edit the movie clip. To add a scratch, create a keyframe where you want the scratch to appear. Select the Pencil tool; use a white .25 stroke and make sure Object Drawing is off. Then draw a small scratch. Create a new keyframe and change the shape of the scratch slightly. Keep adjusting the scratches so that they're a little different for each frame. This isn't a difficult task, but it can be time-consuming. To save time, you can select a random keyframe, hold down the Alt (Windows) or Option (Mac OS) key, and drag the keyframe to a new frame to duplicate it.

4. Add Lines and Flickering

Old movies don't play steadily, either. Lines jump across frames, and the light flickers. You can create both effects. First, unlock and select the Lines layer. I've already created lines in a movie clip. To add a line, select the Line tool. Use a white .25 stroke, and draw a line. Convert it to a movie clip symbol **A**, and then choose Alpha from the Color menu in the Properties Inspector, and drop its opacity to 20%. Then, add a keyframe and create a motion tween, so that the line jumps around a little. Stagger the lines to start and end at different points; the movie clip will loop continuously **B**.

For a flickering effect, on a new layer, create a gray box the size of the stage. Convert it to a movie clip symbol. Choose Brightness from the Color menu in the Properties Inspector. Set the Brightness to 43% **C**. On the next frame, set the Brightness to 72%. It will loop back and forth to create the flickering you see in old-time movies. ▦

T I P

Automatic Sizing. Don't worry about resizing the video component. If Match Source FLV Dimensions is selected in the Content Path dialog box, the component will automatically shrink or grow to match the size of the video.

Skinning Video Components

You can change the appearance of the playback controls for videos in your Flash files.

Apply a Skin to a Video

A skin determines the look and feel of the playback controls on a video. Flash Professional 8 includes dozens of skins for you to choose from, or you can design your own.

To chose a skin, first select the video component on the stage. Then, in the Components Inspector, select the Skin field and click the magnifying glass. In the Select Skin dialog box, choose a skin. You can preview the skins in the dialog box. Click OK when you've found the one you want to use.

Skins have different appearances (steel, mohave, clear, and arctic), different positions (over, which is on top of the video, and external, which is outside the video), and different combinations of controls (play, volume, mute, seek).

When you publish a video with a skin, be sure to upload the .swf file of the skin in the same folder as the Flash file, or the skin won't appear.

Custom Skin

You can create a custom skin using graphics you draw yourself or import from other applications. Flash stores the .swf files of its skins in a Skins folder, and the .fla files for the same skins in the SkinFLA folder. The Skins and SkinFLA folders are in the Macromedia/Flash 8/En/Configuration folder on most computers. (In Windows, the Macromedia folder is in the Program Files folder; in Mac OS, it's in the Applications folder.)

You can modify the .fla file for a skin in Flash. Choose File > Open, and navigate to the SkinFLA folder. Then open the file that is closest to the skin you want to create. For example, it's easiest to select the skin that's in the same position and has the same options. The Flash document contains the skin and all the buttons in all their rollover states.

Import any new graphics you want to use into the library, or draw shapes and convert them to symbols. Then, replace any objects you want to replace. Each button in the default skin is part of a larger symbol, and you may need to double-click several times to get to the symbol you want to replace.

When you've finished customizing the skin, save the Flash file with a new name in the SkinsFLA folder, and then publish the skin as a .swf file and move it to the Skins folder. Now it will appear in the list any time you can select a skin. ▥

COLIN SMITH

Creating Video Silhouettes

Think Apple's iPod commercials are cool? You can create the same effect using video that's been masked with an alpha channel.

1. Prepare the Stage

Open a new file or an existing document that you want to add the silhouette to. Change the background color to let your silhouette stand out; I'm choosing a lime green. Then, increase the frame rate to 30 fps for smoother video playback.

2. Import the Video

Choose File > Import > Import Video. In the Import Video wizard, select the movie you want to use. I'll use Dance short.flv off the How to Wow CD. Select the option for progressive download, and choose None for the skin. Click Finish, and Flash imports the file. Of course, on the stage it just looks like a video component. Test it to see the video.

3. Darken the Subjects in the Video

Right now, we see Christie dancing against a bright green background. But we want to see her silhouette. We need to apply color options, and to do that, we need to convert the video to a movie clip symbol. Select it and press F8. Select Movie Clip for the symbol type.

Now, select the movie clip, and open the Properties Inspector. Choose Brightness from the Color menu. Reduce the brightness to −100. Test the movie. Now we just have a silhouette dancing against a bright background.

Adding Sound to a Button

Add a satisfying clicking sound—or any other sound you create—to your buttons.

1. Import the Sound

In Flash, you can use sounds you create or royalty-free sounds that are available online (soundrangers.com). Flash can support sounds in WAV, AIFF, MP3, and a few other formats. To import a sound, choose File > Import > Import to Library, and select the sound file.

Import the sound once, and you can use it multiple times in the project. I've opened the Button_sound_before.fla file from the How to Wow CD. It's already got a sound file called Click.aif in the library.

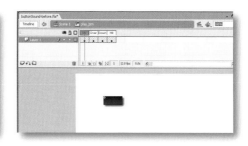

2. Add the Sound to the Down State

Drag the button from the library onto the stage. Double-click the button symbol to edit it. There are four rollover states. They already have drop shadows applied so that the button appears to depress when it's clicked, but there's no sound attached to them yet. We want the clicking sound to occur when the button is pressed, so we need to attach it to the

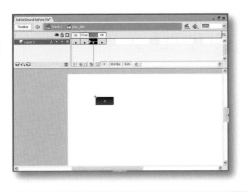

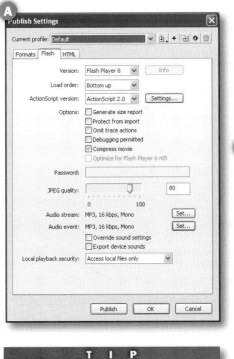

Down state. Select the keyframe for the Down state, and open the Properties Inspector. Choose the Click. aif file from the Sound menu. (All the sounds currently in the library appear in that menu.) Then, choose Event from the Sync menu so that the sound plays all at once, when the event occurs. Flash adds the sound icon to the Down keyframe.

3. Optimize the Sound, If Necessary

Press Ctrl+Enter (Windows) or Cmd+ Return (Mac OS) to test the file. Click the button; you hear a clicking sound. You can change the quality of the sound if you like.

Default audio settings are in the Publish Settings dialog box **A**. Click on the document and then click Settings next to Publish in the Properties Inspector. Select the Flash tab. Click Set next to the Audio Event settings, and change the quality and speed of the sound in the Sound Settings dialog box. Alternatively, you could double-click the sound file in the library, choose a different setting from the Compression menu, and specify the sound quality. You can click the Test button in the Sound Properties dialog box to test the sound immediately **B**. This is also where you can optimize the individual sound. ⬛

T I P

Add Sound Once. If you're using multiple buttons that are all instances of the same symbol, you only need to add the sound to one of them.

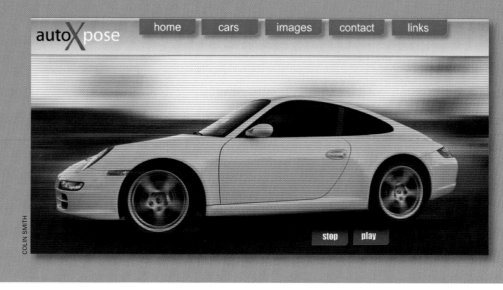

COLIN SMITH

Adding Background Music to a Website

When the page opens, the music starts and continues until the user decides to stop it.

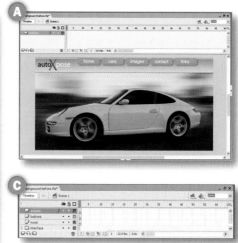

1. Prepare the Document

We'll set up this document so that it's ready for us to add sound and buttons to control that sound. I've opened the Loopingsound-before.fla file from the How to Wow CD **A**. This file already has a website interface in place, and just needs some background sound. Let's import the sound file. Choose File > Import > Import to Library. Select the file called colinGroove.mp3 from the How to Wow CD **B**.

Add three layers to the Timeline, and make sure they're not in the Interface folder. Call the first layer Actions, the second layer Buttons, and the third layer Music **C**.

2. Add Sound to the File

The sound file is in the Library, but we want to add to its own movie clip symbol. Select the Music layer and lock all the other layers. Then choose Insert > New Symbol. Select Movie Clip for the type and name it Music. When you click OK, Flash opens the empty movie clip so you can edit it.

Select the first frame in the Timeline **A**. In the Properties Inspector, choose colinGroove from the Sound menu **B**. Flash adds a blue soundwave to the keyframe, indicating that a sound is attached to it. Now, choose Start from the Sync menu, because we want the music to play as the movie starts. Choose Loop from the next menu so that the music will play continuously.

First, we need to add the frames for the sound file. This .wav file is 193 frames long, so select frame 193 and press F5 to add frames. Now, we want the first frame to be empty so that we can have Flash go to that frame if the viewer wants to stop the music. Double-click to select the entire .wav file in the Timeline, and then drag the entire thing one frame forward. There's an empty keyframe in the first frame **C**.

We've attached the sound to the symbol, but we still need to attach the symbol to the stage. Return to Scene 1 drag the Music symbol from the library onto the stage. Now when you start playing the movie, the music plays.

3. Adjust the Volume

Test the file by pressing Ctrl+Enter (Windows) or Cmd+Return (Mac OS). It plays, but it's a bit loud. We'll drop the volume so that it's more appropriate for a background sound, and to keep from startling our visitors, we'll start out even quieter and gradually fade in.

Double-click the movie clip and select the second frame. Choose Custom from the Effects menu in the Properties Inspector **A**. Flash opens the Edit Envelope dialog box, which lets you control the volume of the sound's right and left channels. Drag the envelope handles to move the envelope lines down well below the center line **B**;

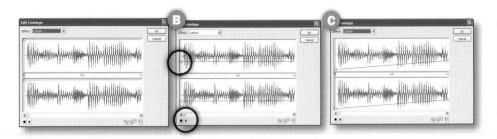

click the Play button at the bottom of the dialog box to test the volume and keep adjusting until the volume seems appropriate for background music.

Then, to fade the sound in, click the right end of the envelope line to create a new handle. Then drag the left envelope handle in each channel to the bottom-left corner, so that the sound gradually builds over time **C**. Click OK, and then test the movie again.

The music slowly fades in, and it's at a reasonable volume.

INSIGHT

Stream for Long Sounds. Stream is a good option if you're playing entire songs or long sound objects, or if you're playing a speech—anything that will take a long time to download. When you choose Stream, Flash will begin to play the sound before it's finished downloading. There's no need to stream a short sound clip like the one we're using here.

4. Create Buttons to Control Audio

There are many reasons a viewer might not want to have background music playing, so we need to provide a way to stop the music. We also need to create a way to restart the music. We'll add buttons to the lower-right section of the stage.

Return to Scene 1. Drag a button from the library onto the stage, and then hold down the Alt (Windows) or Option (Mac OS) key to drag out a second instance of it. For expediency's sake, I'm using the same buttons I used on the main interface, though you'd usually create something less obtrusive. Select the first button and name the instance stopMusic in the Properties Inspector. Select the second and name the instance startMusic. While we're naming instances, select the movie clip that contains the music and name its instance loops.

So that the viewer will know what the buttons are for, let's add simple labels to them. Create a new layer called Labels. Using the Text tool, type "stop" and "play" on the buttons.

```
stopMusic.onRelease=function(){
    loops.gotoAndStop(1);
    stopAllSounds();
}
```

```
stopMusic.onRelease=function(){
    loops.gotoAndStop(1);
    stopAllSounds();
}
startMusic.onRelease=function(){
    loops.gotoAndPlay(2);
}
```

5. Create ActionScript to Control the Buttons

We have the sound and the buttons. Now we just need to add the Action-Script to control the buttons. Select the first frame of the Actions layer and open the Actions panel. We're going to refer to the stopMusic, startMusic, and loops instances. First, we'll have the stop button (stopMusic), when clicked (onRelease), perform the function of going to that first empty frame (1) of the music movie clip (loops) and stopping there (gotoAndStop).

To do that, type

```
stopMusic.onRelease=function(){
    loops.gotoAndStop(1);
}
```

Test this by pressing Ctrl+Enter (Windows) or Cmd+Return (Mac OS). The music keeps playing. We need to tell Flash to stop playing all sounds. So add this line to the script:

```
stopAllSounds();
```

The stop button works now, but we haven't scripted the play button yet.

Return to the Actions panel. This time, we want the play button (startMusic), when clicked (onRelease) to perform a function to go to the second frame (2) of the music movie clip (loops) and play it (gotoAndPlay).

To accomplish that, type

```
startMusic.onRelease=function(){
    loops.gotoAndPlay(2);
}
```

Test the file again. The music plays as the file opens. When you click the stop button, it stops. Click the play button and the music fades back in again. ▥

9

DYNAMIC APPLICATIONS

Extending the functionality of your projects with dynamic content

VARIABLES *206*

CREATING BUTTONS WITH MEMORY *207*

XML PHOTO GALLERY *212*

SCROLLING DYNAMIC TEXT *216*

MP3 MUSIC PLAYER *219*

VALIDATING EMAIL FORM *221*

DESIGNERS AND PROGRAMMERS have used Flash to create some pretty advanced applications on websites. Perhaps you have wondered how they are done and then, upon seeing the code, you have gotten cold chills and decided to settle for something less. Well, I'm going to give you a headstart on the advanced uses of Flash. All the projects in this chapter are designed to make your life easy. I've included dynamic applications that are easy to install and use, ready for you to incorporate into your site.

This chapter gives you a shortcut to useful applications that you may not have access to otherwise. It includes a few of my favorites, and my friend Matt Keefe has also supplied a couple of great examples. Both of us show you all the code and hold nothing back. You will be using ActionScript, PHP, and XML in this chapter. Even if you have never used these things before, you will be able to complete all the lessons.

We start by explaining what variables are, to give you a grounding for the rest of the chapter, which relies heavily on variables in ActionScript.

You will create visited states for buttons in Flash movies, emulating an HTML browser. When a button is clicked, Flash remembers that it's been visited and your visitors will know where they've been.

You can add an elegant photo gallery to your website. The gallery uses XML to load the images, so you can update it without even opening Flash; just upload your image and change a couple of lines in the XML file in a text editor. With the ActionScript we provide, Flash even knows how many photos are supposed to be in the gallery and adjusts the length to suit.

In another project, you'll import text dynamically from an external file. You can edit the file in a text editor, and Flash will pick up the pages automatically. You'll add a scrollbar to the text box that appears only when it's needed. Dynamic scrolling text is the Holy Grail of paragraph text in Flash, and you'll be amazed that it's so easy to add to your web pages.

We'll also give you a form visitors can use to communicate with you without ever leaving your site. With this form, you don't have to post your email address; with no @ signs or "mailto"

tags, spammers can't harvest your address.

Provide a little music for your guests with the MP3 digital jukebox I built for an entertainment company on the web. You can customize it and load your own songs (or speeches, or any other sound objects), so that visitors can choose what they listen to. The track's title and artist name scrolls across a marquee to show you what's playing.

Although some of the ActionScript may be beyond your scripting comfort level, we have made every effort to make the projects in this chapter accessible to everyone. Where the script is easy, I walk you through the creation. Where the project is more complex, I show you how to install and customize it.

Stand out in the marketplace with a fresh identity package. Good commercial design is based on a mixture of science and art. How do you want the world to see your company or organization?

Invest in these services:
Logo development
Stationary packages
Signage

Name	
Email*	
Message	
Phone	
Fax	

* denotes required field   Submit

Variables

Variables let you write ActionScript more efficiently, and give you greater flexibility.

Using Variables

```
1  var weather;
2  weather = "hot";
3  trace(weather);
```

▼ Output

`hot`

Remember learning algebra? In an equation, a variable serves as a placeholder for some other value. The same is true in ActionScript. A variable is a container, standing in for a value. You can use the same variable several times through an ActionScript, but change the value of the variable as many times as you want. This flexibility allows you to record the viewer's actions, such as clicking a link, or change behavior based on whether a condition is true or false. In fact, you can update a variable repeatedly if you keep score in a Flash game or use a counter for some other purpose.

When you first introduce, or declare, a variable in ActionScript, you should assign an initial value to it. You can then use the variable without further defining it, or you can change the value later in the ActionScript.

To declare a variable, type var followed by the variable name, and then define the variable. For example, if the variable is named "weather," and its initial value is "hot," you would type

```
var  weather;
weather = "hot";
```

Let's test the variable by using the trace command. When we run the movie, the output panel will display the value of the variable, "hot".

Data Types

```
1  var weather:String= "It is cold now";
2  trace(weather);
```

▼ Output

`It is cold now`

In ActionScript 2, you assign a data type to a variable when you create it. There are several data types, among them: string, number, and Boolean. A string is text that you want Flash to recognize as a set of characters. When you specify a number data type, Flash won't accept a value for the variable that isn't a number. A Boolean variable is either true or false; Boolean variables are very useful for creating conditional actions. Other popular types are Object and MovieClip.

To declare a data type, add a colon and the data type to the variable name. Let's return to our variable called weather. We want the variable to have a string for a value. So, we can change the initial line to

```
var weather:String
```

Instead of creating another line, let's define the variable right away.

Flash prints "It is cold now" on the screen. ▦

COLIN SMITH

Creating Buttons with Memory

Script buttons to change appearance after they've been clicked.

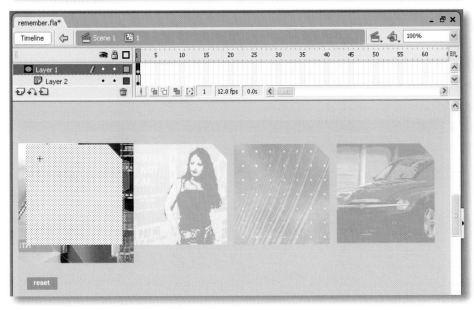

1. Create the Buttons

It's customary on websites for the links that have been clicked to change color. You can provide your viewers with the same information about buttons, so that once a button has been clicked, it appears different on the screen.

First, of course, you need to create your buttons, and create the basic rollover states you want to use with them. I've created the Remember.fla file. The four buttons in this project are instances of movie clip symbols, and the rollover states will be defined in ActionScript. Each button has two layers: one layer contains the image, and the other layer contains a button-shaped mask.

Select each button and give it an instance name in the Properties Inspector. I've named these buttons btn1, btn2, btn3, and btn4. These buttons have been initially set to 75% alpha in the Properties Inspector.

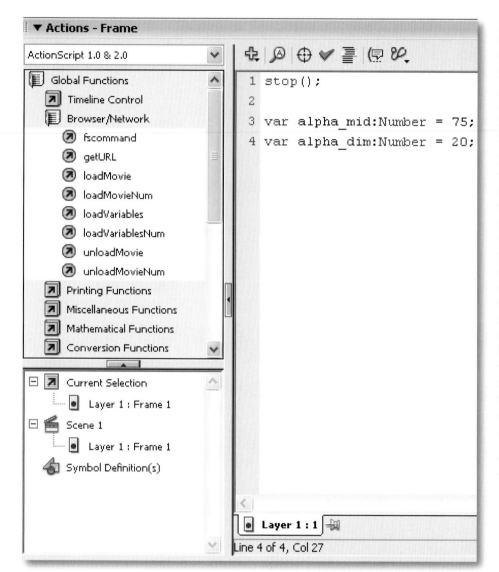

2. Declare Variables in ActionScript

Once the buttons are set up, we're ready to write the ActionScript. Select the first frame on the Timeline, and open the Actions panel. We want to create a stop action first, so that Flash stops on that first keyframe and waits for the viewer to do something. Type stop();

Now, we'll declare our variables. We want a button to dim after it's been selected, so it's obvious to viewers which pages they've visited and which they haven't. We'll create a variable for the buttons that haven't been selected, which we're displaying at 75% opacity, and one for those that have, which we'll display at 20% opacity. Because we use the alpha value in Flash to specify opacity, we'll name the variables alpha_mid and alpha_dim. And we'll give them both the number data type, because we're giving them numerical values: 75 and 20. (We already set the inital value to 75% in the Properties Inspector f or consistency.)

To declare the variables, then, type

```
var alpha_mid:Number=75;
var alpha_dim:Number=20;
```

TIP

Avoiding Repetition. We could have typed the full function for each button separately in this ActionScript, but since the function is identical, we can save space and time by typing just the instance name, the event, and the equal sign for all but the last button.

3. Create the Rollover Action

We want to create several actions for these buttons, based on the viewer's behavior. When the viewer rolls over the button, we want it to appear 100% opaque. When the viewer clicks the button, we want Flash to remember that the button has been clicked and then to display it at 20% opacity.

First, we'll create the over state, so that when the mouse rolls over a button, it has an alpha value of 100%. We've done this in earlier lessons in this book.

```
btn1.onRollOver =
btn2.onRollOver =
btn3.onRollOver =
btn4.onRollOver= function() {
    this._alpha = 100;
}
```

```
1  stop();
2
3  var alpha_mid:Number = 75;
4  var alpha_dim:Number = 20;
5
6
7  btn1.onRollOver =
8  btn2.onRollOver =
9  btn3.onRollOver =
10 btn4.onRollOver= function() {
11     this._alpha = 100;
12 }
```

4. Script the Visited State

Now we need to set up a couple of different scenarios. If the mouse rolls away from the button without clicking it, we want to return to the 75% opacity. If the mouse has clicked the button, though, we want it to change to 20% opacity. We need Flash to evaluate whether the button has been clicked and act accordingly.

Let's create a variable called visited, which will start with a false value. When the button is clicked, the value will change to true, and when the visited value is true, the button's alpha setting should be the value in the alpha_dim variable.

```
btn1.onRelease =
btn2.onRelease =
btn3.onRelease =
btn4.onRelease = function() {
    this.visited = true;
    this._alpha = alpha_dim;
}
```

```
1  stop();
2
3  var alpha_mid:Number = 75;
4  var alpha_dim:Number = 20;
5
6
7  btn1.onRollOver =
8  btn2.onRollOver =
9  btn3.onRollOver =
10 btn4.onRollOver= function() {
11     this._alpha = 100;
12 }
13
14 btn1.onRelease =
15 btn2.onRelease =
16 btn3.onRelease =
17 btn4.onRelease = function() {
18     this.visited = true;
19     this._alpha = alpha_dim;
20 }
```

```
btn1.onRollOut =
btn2.onRollOut =
btn3.onRollOut =
btn4.onRollOut = function() {
    if(this.visited) {
        this._alpha = alpha_dim;
    } else {
        this._alpha = alpha_mid;
    }
}

btn1.onRelease =
btn2.onRelease =
btn3.onRelease =
btn4.onRelease = function() {
    this.visited = true;
    this._alpha = alpha_dim;
}
```

T I P

Alpha Value. To specify an alpha, or opacity, value in ActionScript, use _alpha. Higher alpha values are more visible; lower alpha values are more transparent. Range is 0 to 100.

T I P

Add More Buttons. Just add a line with the instance name for the button each time the buttons are listed in the script. You can add as many buttons as you want.

Now we need to to have Flash evaluate whether visited is true or false when the mouse rolls away from the button. We'll use an if-else conditional statement to do that. So, at the point that it rolls out, if it's been visited, the alpha value is set to alpha_dim, which we defined as 20%. Otherwise, it's set to alpha_mid, which we defined as 75%.

```
btn1.onRollOut =
btn2.onRollOut =
btn3.onRollOut =
btn4.onRollOut = function() {
    if(this.visited) {
        this._alpha = alpha_dim;
    } else {
        this._alpha =
        alpha_mid;
    }
}
```

Once a button has been clicked, it will appear at 20% opacity until the page is closed refreshed or the reset button is clicked.

```
1  stop();
2
3  var alpha_mid:Number = 75;
4  var alpha_dim:Number = 20;
5
6  btn1.onRollOver =
7  btn2.onRollOver =
8  btn3.onRollOver =
9  btn4.onRollOver= function() {
10     this._alpha = 100;
11 }
12
13 btn1.onRollOut =
14 btn2.onRollOut =
15 btn3.onRollOut =
16 btn4.onRollOut = function() {
17     if(this.visited) {
18         this._alpha = alpha_dim;
19     } else {
20         //normal alpha
21         this._alpha = alpha_mid;
22     }
23 }
24
25 btn1.onRelease =
26 btn2.onRelease =
27 btn3.onRelease =
28 btn4.onRelease = function() {
29     this.visited = true;
30     this._alpha = alpha_dim;
31 }
32
33 refresh_btn.onRelease = function(){
34     btn1._alpha=
35     btn2._alpha =
36     btn3._alpha =
37     btn4._alpha = alpha_mid;
38     btn1.visited= btn2.visited = btn3.visited = btn4.visited = false;
39
40 }
```

5. Create a Reset Button

If you want viewers to be able to reset the buttons so that they're all at 75% opacity, you can add a reset button to the page. I created one in the Remember.fla file. It has the instance name Refresh_btn.

When the viewer clicks the reset button, we want all the buttons to return to 75% opacity, and we want the visited value to return to false.

So, script the reset button (Refresh_btn), when clicked (onRelease) to have the function of setting the _alpha value for each button to alpha_mid (which we defined at 75%) and to set the visited value to false for each button. If we didn't reset the variable for the visited state, the buttons would return to 20% opacity when the user rolls their mouse out.

```
refresh_btn.onRelease = function(){
    btn1._alpha=
    btn2._alpha =
    btn3._alpha =
    btn4._alpha = alpha_mid;
    btn1.visited= btn2.visited
= btn3.visited = btn4.visited =
false;

}
```

Now, when we click the reset button, all the buttons return to their original state, ready for more interaction. ▥

COLIN SMITH

XML Photo Gallery

Adapt this photo gallery, which uses XML to import the images, to show off your own photos.

Contributed by Matt Keefe.

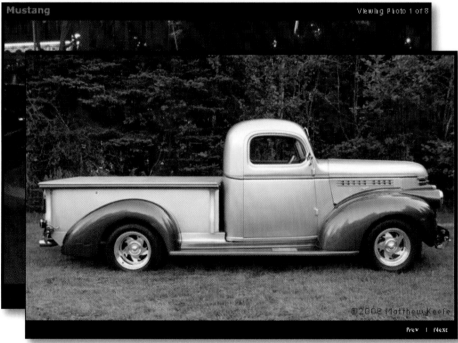

MATT KEEFE

1. Get Acquainted with the Gallery

In Chapter 6, we created a fairly simple photo gallery, scripting thumbnail buttons to load images. This gallery, created by Matt Keefe of ScriptPlayground.com, is more elegant and easier to update. The ActionScript code is a bit complex, but you don't need to understand it to use this gallery on your site.

Several files are required to modify and publish the gallery; you'll find the files on the How to Wow CD. The Gallery_finished.fla file is the Flash file you can edit. The Gallery_finished. swf file is the published Flash file; you'll replace it with your own if you make any edits to the Flash document. The Gallery_list.xml file is an XML document created in a text editor or an application such as Dreamweaver. The fullsize_images folder contains the images displayed in the gallery; it currently contains eight images.

Run the Gallery_finished.swf file to see what the gallery looks like. In addition to the image itself, there's a caption for the image, a line that reports which

MATT KEEFE

image you're viewing and how many total images there are, and buttons to move to the previous and next images. The Prev button is dimmed when you're viewing the first image, and the Next button is dimmed when you're viewing the last. When you click Next, the next image gradually becomes more visible.

Because we're using XML, you can add or remove images without even opening Flash. The sequence number will automatically update to display how many images there are. XML code is similar to HTML, and you can open the XML file in any application that can read and save text-only files; save the file with an XML extension.

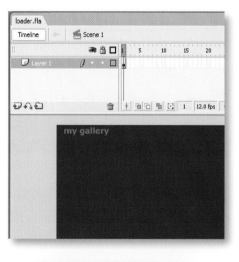

2. Load the Gallery into Your Flash Document

To use the gallery in your own pages, you need to load it into a Flash document or a website. Create a new Flash document with a gray background, and add a heading using the text tool. I've typed "my gallery" at the top. Make sure the heading is static text, not dynamic text, in the Properties Inspector, and select your font, type size, and text color.

Save the Flash document in the same folder as the XML file. Name the file Loader.fla.

We'll load the gallery into an empty movie clip, as we've done before. Insert a new symbol called myloader. Return to Scene 1. Drag the movie clip from the library onto the stage, and position it on the left edge, beneath the header. Name the instance loader_mc.

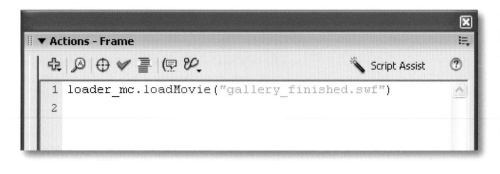

```
1  loader_mc.loadMovie("gallery_finished.swf")
2
```

Select the first frame and then open the Actions panel. We'll type a simple script here to load the gallery. We'll call on the loader_mc instance to load the gallery movie.

```
loader_mc.loadMovie(
"gallery_finished.swf")
```

Test the script by pressing Ctrl+Enter (Windows) or Cmd+Return (Mac OS). The gallery loads into the empty movie clip.

T I P

Load on Demand. We're loading the gallery immediately, but you could attach the loader to a button and create a function to load it when the button is clicked.

3. Add Your Own Images

Matt's images are lovely, but you have your own photographs to show off. Copy your images into the Fullsize Images folder and delete the ones that are already there.

Now, we need to make a few changes to the XML file. Open it in Dreamweaver, Notepad, or another application that can save in text-only format. Each image has its own node, surrounded by <image> tags. The first line contains the caption, and the second line contains the file name.

For example, this is a node:

```
<image>
    <name>Private Jet</name>
    <image>image_08.jpg</image>
</image>
```

Replace the caption and file name for each image. If you're including more than eight images, copy and paste the node as many times as you need to, and include the caption and file name for each image. I'll add a photo with the caption "Sunset at the Beach." Save the file as a text-only file with an .XML extension. Run the Gallery_finished.swf file again. Now your photos appear in the gallery, and it automatically knows how many images there are.

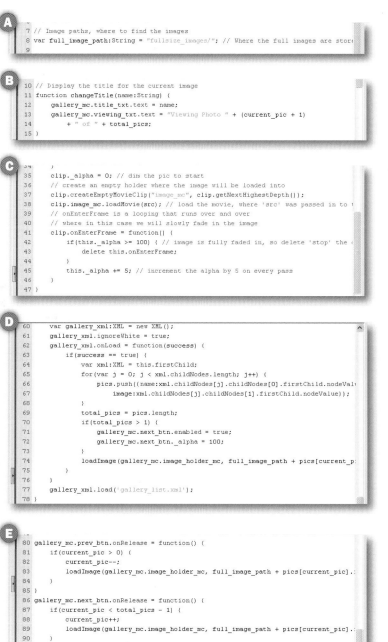

A

```
7   // Image paths, where to find the images
8   var full_image_path:String = "fullsize_images/"; // Where the full images are store
9
```

B

```
10  // Display the title for the current image
11  function changeTitle(name:String) {
12      gallery_mc.title_txt.text = name;
13      gallery_mc.viewing_txt.text = "Viewing Photo " + (current_pic + 1)
14          + " of " + total_pics;
15  }
```

C

```
34      }
35      clip._alpha = 0; // dim the pic to start
36      // create an empty holder where the image will be loaded into
37      clip.createEmptyMovieClip("image_mc", clip.getNextHighestDepth());
38      clip.image_mc.loadMovie(src); // load the movie, where 'src' was passed in to
39      // onEnterFrame is a looping that runs over and over
40      // where in this case we will slowly fade in the image
41      clip.onEnterFrame = function() {
42          if(this._alpha >= 100) { // image is fully faded in, so delete 'stop' the
43              delete this.onEnterFrame;
44          }
45          this._alpha += 5; // increment the alpha by 5 on every pass
46      }
47  }
```

D

```
60      var gallery_xml:XML = new XML();
61      gallery_xml.ignoreWhite = true;
62      gallery_xml.onLoad = function(success) {
63          if(success == true) {
64              var xml:XML = this.firstChild;
65              for(var j = 0; j < xml.childNodes.length; j++) {
66                  pics.push((name:xml.childNodes[j].childNodes[0].firstChild.nodeValu
67                      image:xml.childNodes[j].childNodes[1].firstChild.nodeValue));
68              }
69              total_pics = pics.length;
70              if(total_pics > 1) {
71                  gallery_mc.next_btn.enabled = true;
72                  gallery_mc.next_btn._alpha = 100;
73              }
74              loadImage(gallery_mc.image_holder_mc, full_image_path + pics[current_p
75          }
76      }
77      gallery_xml.load('gallery_list.xml');
78  }
```

E

```
80  gallery_mc.prev_btn.onRelease = function() {
81      if(current_pic > 0) {
82          current_pic--;
83          loadImage(gallery_mc.image_holder_mc, full_image_path + pics[current_pic].
84      }
85  }
86  gallery_mc.next_btn.onRelease = function() {
87      if(current_pic < total_pics - 1) {
88          current_pic++;
89          loadImage(gallery_mc.image_holder_mc, full_image_path + pics[current_pic].
90      }
91  }
```

4. Upload the Gallery Files

To use the gallery on your website, upload the Loader.swf file, the Gallery_finished.swf file, the Gallery_list.xml file, and the Fullsize Images folder to your server.

Here is a brief explaination of what the code does.

First, we load variables to identify the current picture and the total number of pictures. We load a variable to create an array for the pictures themselves. We also load a variable called full_image_path, and define that path. In the future, if you want to change the path, you only have to change it in one place and the script will still work **A**.

The next section finds the caption from the XML file and displays both the caption and the sequence number **B**. Then, we have a function that loads the image and gradually changes its alpha value from 0 to 100% **C**. The next section determines whether the prev and next buttons should be enabled for the particular image in the sequence. Then the XML gallery is loaded, and Flash looks at the information inside the nodes, called children **D**. Finally, the prev and next buttons are scripted to load the previous or next image **E**. ▥

Stand out in the marketplace with a fresh identity package. Good commercial design is based on a mixture of science and art. How do you want the world to see your company or organization?

Invest in these services:
Logo development
Stationary packages
Signage

Scrolling Dynamic Text

Import text dynamically and include scroll bars if it's larger than its text box.

---

id.txt - Notepad

File   Edit   Format   View   Help

```
Pitch=<html><body><b>Identity</b>
Stand out in the marketplace with a fresh ident
Good commercial design is based on a mixture of

<b>Invest in these services:</b>
Logo development
Stationary packages
Signage□Convention Identity
Collateral identity

Don't cut corners when it comes to your image.
</body></html>
```

1. Prepare the External Text File

We want Flash to import a text file and display it on the stage, adding a scroll bar if the text is larger than the box we create to contain it. First, we need to create the external text file. You can use any text editor, but the key is to make sure it's truly a TXT file, without formatting applied such as RTF. If you're using Windows, Notepad is a good choice. If you're working in Mac OS, use SimpleText or Stickies. Word will also work.

Type the text. The first line should include the variable name that you'll use to call the text and the "=" assignment operator. I've used the variable name "pitch" here. If you want to format the text, include HTML tags in the text, as I've done. When you save the file, make sure you save it as a text file (with a .txt extension). Save it in the same folder as your Flash file, and remember the name of the file!

2. Create the Text Box in Flash

Now we need to create the text box that this text will flow into. Open the Flash document. Select the Text tool. Choose Dynamic Text in the Properties Inspector, because we want Flash to pull in whatever text is assigned to the variable; we won't be typing the text into this box ourselves. Now drag the Text tool to create the text box. Choose a font, type size, and other formatting options for the text that will appear in the text box. _sans or _serif will produce a consistent look across platforms.

There are a few options to set up. Choose Multiline so that the text will wrap and fill the text box. If you want viewers to be able to select and copy the text, click the Selectable icon **A**. If you used HTML tags in your text file, select the Render Text as HTML icon **B**. If you want the edges of the text box to show, select the Show Border Around Text icon **C**.

Name the instance, so we can refer to it in ActionScript, click with the select tool. I've named it textbox in my file.

3. Add a UI Scroll Bar Component

If the text is too large for the text box, we want Flash to provide a scroll bar; if the text fits in the text box, we don't want the scroll bar to appear. Flash makes this part super-easy. There's a ready-made component that does just what we want to do.

Open the Components panel. Expand the User Interface options. Then, drag the UIScrollBar component onto the stage. Release it at the right side inside the text box, and it will snap to the side. Now, if it's needed, the scroll bar will be there; if it's not, it won't. I told you it was easy!

T I P

HTML Text. If you're not using HTML text, just type `textbox.text=this.Pitch;` instead of `textbox.htmlText=this.Pitch;`.

T I P

Moving the File. We've put the text file in the same folder as the Flash file to keep things simpler. You can store the text file in a different folder, but if you do, be sure to write the path in the script using either dot notation or forward slashes. For example, if you store the text file in a folder called Text, the last line in the script would read

`myVars.load("text/id.txt");` or
`myVars.load("text.id.txt")`

```
myVars = new LoadVars();
myVars.onLoad = function(){
     textbox.htmlText=this.Pitch.
};
myVars.load("id.txt");
```

---

4. Create Script to Import the Text File

We're ready to write the ActionScript to import and display the text. Select the first frame in the Timeline, and then open the Actions panel.

We want Flash to load the text into the text box we've created. Remember that we're using a variable (pitch) for the text file, and an instance name (textbox) for the text box. The script isn't very long, but it does look a little different than the scripts we've written before.

First, we'll use the LoadVars object to load a variable, and we'll create an instance of it called myVars. Then we'll create a function to be performed when the file is loaded; the function will fill the textbox instance with HTML text, and it will equal the value of the pitch variable. Finally, we'll tell it where to find the document it needs to load. My document is called id.txt. Make sure to include the file extension and put quotation marks around the file name.

```
myVars = new LoadVars();
myVars.onLoad = function(){
     textbox.htmlText=this.
     Pitch;
};
myVars.load("id.txt");
```

Test the file by pressing Ctrl+Enter (Windows) or Cmd+Return (Mac OS). The text loads with HTML formatting, if you've included it, and the scroll bar appears so you can scroll through the text. ▥

---

text-end.swf

File View Control Debug

Stand out in the marketplace with a fresh identity package. Good commercial design is based on a mixture of science and art. How do you want the world to see your company or organization?

Invest in these services:
Logo development
Stationary packages
Signage

MP3 Music Player

Put a jukebox on your website so your visitors can play your favorite tunes.

1. Create the Jukebox Interface

I've created a small digital jukebox in the Music_player.fla file on the How to Wow CD. You're welcome to use this interface in your own projects, or you can design your own interface. The song title scrolls across the bottom of the jukebox; if no song is selected, the text prompts you to select one. When you click a number, the corresponding song plays. Click Stop to stop the music.

The jukebox has six invisible buttons; each button has an instance name. The numbered buttons are btn1, btn2, and so on. The stop button is named stop. We're using the empty movie clip called m_mc (for music movie clip) as a container to load the music files, which are published as SWFs.

B ▼ Library - music1.fla

music1.fla

4 items

Name	Type
colinGroove.mp3	Sound
marquee	Movie C
music	Movie c
Tween 1	Graphic

A music_player.fla* music1.fla*

Timeline Scene 1

Layer 4
Layer 3

1 30.0 fps 0.0s

C

Sound: colinGroove.mp3

Effect: None Edit...

Sync: Stream Loop

44 kHz Stereo 16 Bit 16.1 s 128.5 kB

2. Prepare the Music Files

Each song is in a separate Flash document. Each has two layers, one for the music itself and one a mask for the marquee **A**. There are two clips in the library, one for the music and one for the marquee text. Additionally, the music file itself is in the library.

To use a different song, choose File > Import to Library, and then select the MP3 file you want to import **B**. Then, select the first frame in Layer 1, and choose the new song from the Sound menu in the Properties Inspector **C**.

Double-click the Marquee symbol in the library to edit it, and type the name of the new song. Lastly, publish the revised Flash file, as it's the SWF file that the jukebox will look for.

TIP

More than Music. You can use the jukebox to play speech as well as music. For example, you can attach recordings of your children saying adorable things, political leaders delivering inspiring or embarrassing speeches, or even spoken instructions for performing different tasks.

```
onLoad =function(){
    m_mc.loadMovie("music6.swf");
}

btn1.onRelease = function(){
    m_mc.loadMovie("music1.swf");
}
btn2.onRelease = function(){
    m_mc.loadMovie("music2.swf");
}
btn3.onRelease = function(){
    m_mc.loadMovie("music3.swf");
}
btn4.onRelease = function(){
    m_mc.loadMovie("music4.swf");
}
btn5.onRelease = function(){
    m_mc.loadMovie("music5.swf");
}
btn_stp.onRelease = function(){
    m_mc.loadMovie("music6.swf");
}
```

3. Adapt the Script for Your Site

The ActionScript in the Music_player.fla file is ready to go. There are five buttons for sounds on the jukebox, but there are actually six SWF files. The sixth clip is the stop button. It has no sound file attached to it, and its marquee prompts the viewer to make a selection. The stop button is loaded when the jukebox first loads.

The script is straightforward. The onLoad event in the first line loads the stop button SWF file into the empty movie clip. The rest of the script loads each track's SWF file when its button is selected.

If you're using the jukebox inside another movie clip, include the appropriate path to each instance in the ActionScript.

Validating Email Form

Load this form into your website so that visitors can give you feedback without having to leave your site.

Contributed by Matt Keefe.

1. Adapt the Form in Flash

The email form in the Email_validation.fla file on the How to Wow CD is almost ready to use. Matt Keefe at ScriptPlayground.com was kind enough to provide this form, which you can add to your website. Visitors who want to communicate with you can fill out the fields, click the Submit button, and receive a thank you message. You'll get their message without ever having to publish your email address online, where it's available for spammers to harvest it. And your visitors can communicate with you without leaving your site.

This form has standard fields in it, but you can add or remove fields as necessary. The fields are TextInput components. To add a field, select the Input Boxes layer, drag a TextInput component from the User Interface section of the Components panel **A**, adjust its size, and then choose the appropriate options in the Parameters panel. To let visitors enter text in the field, choose True for Editable.

```
11   var fields:Array = [
12       // Input Field, Validate Function
13       ['name', 'validateName'],
14       ['email', 'validateEmail'],
15       ['msg', 'validateMessage'],
16       ['phone',''],
17       ['fax','']
18   ];
```

If it's not a password field, choose False. Name the instance of the component so you can refer to it in ActionScript. Add a label to it (text that identifies it), so that your visitors know what the field is for. For example, if you want to add a field for a fax number, label it Fax on screen and name the instance fax **A**.

You'll need to make a few changes in the ActionScript to accommodate a new field. Select the first frame in the Actions layer, and open the Actions panel. In the array section that lists all the fields, copy the line from an existing field, paste it, and replace the instance name with the instance name for the new field **B**. (Note that the last entry does not have a comma at the end like the rest of the entries in the array.) Including validation for a field makes it a required field. If you don't want to use validation, add two single quotation marks after the comma.

```
<?php
/*-------------------------------------------------
Author  : www.mkeefedesign.com | Matthew Keefe
Contact : matt@mkeefedesign.com
$Id: send_email.php ,v 1.0 Tue Apr 26, 2005 02:20 PM
-------------------------------------------------
* CODING & DESIGN @2004 mkeefeDESIGN | ALL RIGHTS RESERVED
-------------------------------------------------*/

$recipients = "youremail@yourdomain.com" . ",";
$subject = "The Message";

// The following three variables are gathered from Flash
$name = $_POST['name'];
$email = $_POST['email'];
$message = $_POST['msg'];
$phone = $_POST['phone'];

// Grab todays date
$date = date("F j, Y", time());

// This block is the actual message that is sent in the email
$email_info .= "Below is the visitors contact info and message.\n\n";
$email_info .= "Visitor's Info:\n";
$email_info .= "-------------------------------------------\n";
$email_info .= "Name:   " . $name . "\n";
$email_info .= "Email:   " . $email . "\n";
$email_info .= "Phone:   " . $phone . "\n";
$email_info .= "Date Sent:  " . $date . "\n\n";
$email_info .= "Message\n";
$email_info .= "-------------------------------------------\n";
$email_info .= "" . $message . "\n";

$mailheaders = "From: " . $email . "\n";
$mailheaders .= "Reply-To: " . $email . "\n\n";

if(mail($recipients, $subject, $email_info, $mailheaders)) {
    // Print a success for Flash to know the email is being sent
    print "&success=true";
}
?>
```

2. Modify the PHP File

PHP is a programming language used to produce dynamic web content. You don't have to understand PHP to use this widget. We'll use a PHP file to return the email message, but all you need to know how to do is make a few changes in a text editor.

Open emailvalidation.php in Dreamweaver, Notepad, or any other application that can open a text file. First, replace "youremail@yourdomain. com" with your email address. Your email address needs to be within quotation marks. Then replace "the message" with whatever subject line you want to use.

Those are the only changes you must make to use this email form. However, if you've added or modified the fields, you'll need to make a few more changes.

```php
<?php
/*------------------------------------------------
Author  : www.mkeefedesign.com | Matthew Keefe
Contact : matt@mkeefedesign.com
$Id: send_email.php ,v 1.0 Tue Apr 26, 2005 02:20 PM
------------------------------------------------
* CODING & DESIGN @2004 mkeefeDESIGN | ALL RIGHTS RESERVED
------------------------------------------------*/

$recipients = "youremail@yourdomain.com" . ",";
$subject = "The Message";

// The following three variables are gathered from Flash
$name = $_POST['name'];
$email = $_POST['email'];
$message = $_POST['msg'];
$phone = $_POST['phone'];
$fax = $_POST['fax'];

// Grab todays date
$date = date("F j, Y", time());

// This block is the actual message that is sent in the email
$email_info .= "Below is the visitors contact info and message.\n\n";
$email_info .= "Visitor's Info:\n";
$email_info .= "-------------------------------------------\n";
$email_info .= "Name:  " . $name . "\n";
$email_info .= "Email:  " . $email . "\n";
$email_info .= "Phone:  " . $phone . "\n";
$email_info .= "Fax:  " . $fax . "\n";
$email_info .= "Date Sent:  " . $date . "\n\n";
$email_info .= "Message\n";
$email_info .= "-------------------------------------------\n";
$email_info .= "" . $message . "\n";

$mailheaders = "From: " . $email . "\n";
$mailheaders .= "Reply-To: " . $email . "\n\n";

if(mail($recipients, $subject, $email_info, $mailheaders)) {
    // Print a success for Flash to know the email is being sent
    print "&success=true";
}

?>
```

email_validation.swf

File   View   Control   Debug

Name

Email*

Message

Phone

Fax

* denotes required field   Submit

You'll need to add a variable name for each field. You can copy the line for an existing variable and replace the appropriate instance name.

For example, in the variables section, if you added a fax field in Flash, add this line to the variables section in the PHP file:

```
$fax=$_POST['fax'];
```

Then, to include data from the new field in the message you receive, add a line to that section. You can copy and paste an existing line, and then enter the information for the new field. For example, the fax information might go right beneath the phone information, so the new code would look like this:

```
$email_info .= "Name:  " . $name . "\n";

$email_info .= "Email:  " . $email . "\n";

$email_info .= "Phone:  " . $phone . "\n";

$email_info .= "Fax:  " . $fax . "\n";

$email_info .= "Date Sent:  " . $date . "\n\n";
```

Save the PHP file as a text-only file with a PHP extension.

3. Upload the Files to Your Server

You're ready to go. Just upload the PHP file and the SWF file to the same folder on your server. Make sure that PHP is enabled through your web server. If you're not sure whether PHP is enabled, contact your ISP. ▥

Index

Get Free Flash Training - Right Now

Watch over the Colin's shoulder!

Learn powerful Flash techniques by watching Colin Smith work... just as if you were there.

Learning Flash is now as easy as getting online. Software Cinema and Peachpit Press are pleased to introduce you to the newest and easiest way to master the program. Using new advances in streaming media, we are able to bring you the proven techniques in vivid, full-resolution detail. You will learn quickly and naturally as Colin walks you through each technique as if he were right there with you. As part of purchasing this How to Wow book, you can experience three lessons sampling these dynamic interactive training movies for yourself! Simply go to www.software-cinema.com/htw for log-in instructions.

Colin has a real knack for unlocking the hidden secrets of any application—always with a practical emphasis on quality, flexibility and speed. In this How to Wow training for Software Cinema Colin holds nothing back. It's all here (demonstrated in real time, in full resolution, with great sound) that will get you on the road to building top-notch Flash presentations. From the basics to building inter activity to making your ideas come alive with motion, Workshops-On-Demand and the DVD discs are another teaching tool that will save you time!

See the next page for more information and a discount offer for Flash training that is easy to understand.

NOTE: Specific tutorial movies may differ from the examples shown here

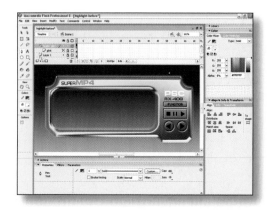
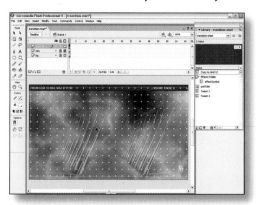
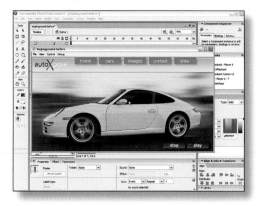

Learn to Work Creatively & Efficiently

You've got the software. Now see the movies!

How to Wow-Mastering Flash: Flash interactive training will guide you step-by-step with an emphasis on uncompromising quality, last-minute flexibility, and go-home-at-night speed. Whether it's learning the basics, making interactivity or designing high-end special effects and motion, learn the tools and techniques that will enable you with How to Wow!

Discs and Workshops appear below... see three lessons free online now!

HOW TO WOW - FUNDAMENTAL FLASH
Chapter 1 : Mastering the Basics
- Symbols
- Frames and Keyframes
- Basic Motion Tween
- Basic Shape Tween
- Symbols and Instances
- Nesting Movie Clips
- Flash Detection
- Animated Filters
- Flash on CD and DVD

Chapter 2 : Creating Imagery
- Hi-Tech Interface
- 3D Buttons
- Thumbnails from Images
- Scan Lines and Patterns
- Make a Web Banner
- Bitmap Caching

Chapter 3 : Alive With Motion
- Motion Blurred Slide-In
- Animated Page Transitions
- Shim of Light on a Logo
- Shimmering Metal
- Freehand Writing
- Motion on a Path
- Unrolling a Scroll

Chapter 4 : Special Effects
- Vector Hand Painted Technique
- Morphing an Outline to an Image
- Creating an Outline the Easy Way
- Optimizing Raster Graphics
- Animated 3D in Flash
- Smoke and Steam
- Reflections

HOW TO WOW - ADVANCED FLASH
Chapter 5 : Character Animation
- Walk Cycles
- Anticipation
- Squash & Stretch
- Hinging - Free Transform, Scale and Object Positioning

Chapter 6 : Adding Interactivity
- Advanced Buttons
- Actionscript
- Custom Animated Preloader
- Custom Graphic Cursor
- Click and Drag
- Photo Gallery with Thumbnails

Chapter 7 : Navigating with Style
- Entire Site in Flash
- Build a Graphical Shell to Load Pages
- Bringing Things into Focus
- Slide-out Menu
- Drop-down Menu

Chapter 8 : Working with Video & Sound
- Keying out Video
- FLV Integration
- Masked Video with Green Screen
- Silhouette Effect
- Vector Video
- Old Scratched Cinema Effect
- Skinning Components
- Add Sound to a Button
- Looping Music with a Mute Button

Chapter 9 : Widgets for Your Use
- Variables
- Buttons that Remember
- Photo Gallery using XML
- Scrolling Dynamic Text
- MP3 Music Player
- Email Form

software CINEMA®